ROADSTERS

ROADSTERS

FIFTY YEARS OF TOP-DOWN SPEED

DON SPIRO

MetroBooks

MetroBooks

An Imprint of Friedman/Fairfax Publishers

ISBN 1-56799-943-3

Editors: Ann Kirby-Payne and Alexandra Bonfante-Warren
Art Director: Kevin Ullrich
Designer: Mark Weinberg
Photography Editor: Kate Perry
Production Manager: Maria Gonzalez

Color separations by Fine Arts Repro House Co., Ltd.
Printed in China by Leefung-Asco Printers Ltd

1 3 5 7 9 10 8 6 4 2

For bulk purchases and special sales, please contact:
Friedman/Fairfax Publishers
Attention: Sales Department
15 West 26th Street
New York, NY 10010
212/685-6610 FAX 212/685-1307

Visit our website:
www.metrobooks.com

CONTENTS

THE ROADSTER EXPERIENCE

Oh, man, the sound—the sucking and wheezing of triple SUs, as that straight six winds up and down, the cut gears of the differential telegraphing in an almost seductive manner mere inches away, through the seat bottom. . . . Back into the seat as 3.8 liters spool up. What torque! Two lanes suddenly widen to six, then eight, then become a gray black swath of parking lot. . . . Out of the turn, throttle nailed to the floor, the sinister wall is a growing sliver of white fear along the left-hand edge of the dashboard. Dunlops strain for grip against centrifugal force heightened by the severe slope of the banking—a force that seems at once to envelop and take hold of the sleek car like a willful child's hand on a Dinky toy. The absurdly skinny wood wheel gives no reassurance in hand, but provides more than enough feedback about what the front end is doing. Concentrate . . . work the throttle . . . control . . . fight the overwhelming "survival" urge to drive the brake pedal through the floorboard and bring an end to this madness. . . . Ah, straightaway at last . . . the back end thankfully senses it too, gathers itself, and dutifully gets back in line with the front end. In spite of the icy wind's roar, all the gears, cams, rods, and combustion explode out the exhaust tip in a soulful harmony born in Coventry and refined on Mulsanne . . . I glance over at Mike, my close friend since kindergarten, and the owner of this exquisite roadster. He's gone catatonic; that smile will take a week to thaw out and go away . . . mine, too!

PAGE 8: *The BMW Z-3 2.8. The Z-3 series, built in the United States, was introduced in 1995. It instantly garnered universal acclaim, and remains BMW's most popular roadster.*

ABOVE: *1950 Ferrari 166mm Touring Barchetta. Designed by Pininfarina and built by Michelotti, the 166mm set a standard that all Ferraris of road or track would follow. Powered by a V12 engine, its goal was simple—to win races—but it was the fact that Enzo Ferrari's designs were commensurate with his cars' performance that made the Ferrari name legendary. With wins at Le Mans and the prestigious Mille Miglia, the 166 proved early on that Ferrari would always be a major contender in racing.*

It's one of those rare driving experiences that you know you'll never have again: three glorious and incredible flat-out laps around Pocono Raceway behind the slender and elegant wheel of a black '67 Jaguar XKE roadster. Those three fleeting laps remain to this day the defining moment, the core from which all other automotive experiences I have had since radiate. Though they rolled off on an overcast and wintry March day twenty-three years ago, in my mind I am fooled countless times into thinking that it was just yesterday.

Great drives in a great automobile stay with you. And great drives in a roadster—top down, wind in your face, all your senses assaulted by the collective elements of what makes a roadster so very special—become an integral part of your soul. Once this experience has been savored, a drive in any other style of automobile, no matter how fast or finely engineered it may be, pales in comparison to the intimacy of two seats and the wide-open sky above.

Standing still, motor off and top down, the XKE is a delight to the eye from any angle and in any light, a benchmark design of the 1960s. In its time one had to look to Maranello, Italy, birthplace and home of Ferrari and legendary design houses like Pininfarina, to find a body design equal to the incredible aesthetics of the XKE design. The marvelous sweeping curves, bulges, tapers, delicate bumpers, and brightwork are at once utilitarian and sensual. The interior is a blend of stitched leather, brushed chrome, a bit of carpeting, plus that skinny, handsome, and wonderfully British wooden steering wheel.

I've been lucky enough to have turned the keys to awaken a slumbering Turbo Porsche flat six, a Lotus or two, numerous Corvettes, and other American muscle cars; once in my life I even had the rare privilege of getting behind the wheel of a Ferrari. As exciting as those moments of ignition were, that wonderful two-step "toggle on/hit starter" that brings to life the XKE remains beyond compare. Of course the sound that followed as 3.8 liters of an in-line, dual overhead cam six-cylinder sprang to life is to this day one of my all-time favorite "exhaust tunes." No in-line six I've ever heard before or since has approached the six in that XKE. I've driven the XKE coupe and the swollen and bulbous Two Plus Two coupe, but for me the *only* Jaguar is the XKE roadster. The XKE is a landmark example of the roadster, that singular breed of automobile.

HISTORIC PRECEDENTS

Roadsters can trace their origins to the decade or so just prior to World War II. In Europe, they were developed as pure racing machines to compete on the most challenging tracks across the continent: Le Mans, Monza, and Avus. Short on amenities and creature comforts, these early roadsters were built for the express purpose of moving as fast as possible in order to win races. The essential design was simple: a roadster was defined by an open cockpit, two seats (for driver and riding mechanic—de rigueur for racing in that period), a highly tuned suspension for road racing, and a state-of-the-art powerplant. Alfa Romeo, Bentley, Mercedes-Benz, and Bugatti are among the legendary names that typify roadsters from the European pre–World War II era. As race-bred machinery, roadsters from such venerable garages were built in extremely low numbers and commanded high prices; thus they remained far out of the driving reach of the general public.

Roadsters also developed in the United States during the same period, and in similarly small numbers. Sure, there were roadsters from Dodge, Ford, Chevrolet, and other mainstream manufacturers, but these were merely two-seat, convertible versions of their standard, everyday passenger cars. In the United States true roadsters were the domain of the rich and famous. Movie stars and starlets, captains of industry, and Gatsby-styled playboys of the 1920s drove custom-bodied roadsters from such legendary and long-gone marques as Duesenberg, Cord, Packard, and Auburn. Built

for different purposes, U.S. roadsters of the period were wickedly fast, but were often twice the size of their European counterparts. They traded the hallmarks of the European breeds—light weight and fine handling—in favor of size and status. In short, these American roadsters were rare icons of success and enormous wealth. To own an Auburn Boat-Tailed Speedster or a Duesenberg SJ meant that you had "arrived" and were comfortably perched at the very top of the economic food chain. There's a wonderful photograph of Gary Cooper, circa 1930, leaning against the fender of his Duesenberg SJ roadster, cigarette in hand, a look of total satisfaction on his face, flush and confident in his success. It is a portrait that epitomizes the roadster experience in the prewar United States.

The Great Depression effectively put an end to the U.S. roadster as well as to high-end roadsters in Europe, as the previously booming economy went bust globally in 1929. Hard on the heels of the Depression came World War II. Over in Europe, as in North America, all nonessential goods and products disappeared during wartime. Yet automobiles, particularly roadsters, reemerged in the immediate postwar period—most notably with the MG-TC—and their popularity soared. U.S. servicemen returning from Europe, especially those who had been stationed in England, brought home their memories of driving small, nimble cars swiftly over charming and challenging English country roads. These memories helped launch and fuel demand for imported roadsters in the postwar United States. By the early 1950s, roadsters were popular enough in the United States to prompt American automakers to launch new, more affordable alternatives to the racing-tuned beauties coming out of Great Britain and Italy. Chevrolet led the way—initially with very limited success—with the introduction, in 1953, of the fiberglass-bodied Corvette. Ford followed suit with its two-seat Thunderbird two years later.

OPEN AIR MEETS OPEN ROAD

Not merely a mode of transportation, the roadster is an experience: the small size, the intimate two-seat-only arrangement, the glory of top-down motoring (whether because of or in spite of the weather) bring driver and road together as few cars can. The level of involvement between driver and car is so heightened by the open air in a roadster that similar coupes—though genetically the same beneath the skin—are completely different creatures. For everyday motoring thrills, there is nothing that is even close to the experience of driving a roadster. A fine roadster can make a mundane run to the convenience store for a carton of low-fat milk an event as highly anticipated as that of the flag-off at the start of the Monte Carlo Rally.

As charming, endearing, exciting, and fun to drive as they were, those early postwar roadsters had certain traits that are perhaps best superseded. Roll-down windows were not part of the package; instead, most of the early roadsters came with a pair of side curtains. Usually made of a sheet of thick, formed plastic to fit in the window opening between the door and canvas top, these "windows" were far from weather-tight; a tight-fitting weather seal was simply out of the question

around the side curtain. What's worse, the plastic scratched easily, so that after a year or so the view out the side of a roadster with the side curtain in place was opaque at best: making a turn into oncoming traffic could be quite an adventure in such a car.

Should a rainstorm suddenly develop while you were out motoring with the top down, you'd find yourself in an even worse predicament. We live in a day and age of convertibles and roadsters whose tops retract and return to place smoothly with the mere push of a dashboard button. This precision and ease of operation offer little inkling of the Herculean effort required to put the top up on an early roadster. First, you had to rig the frame that supported the top into position. Think of an erector set, a Rube Goldberg contraption, and every swear word you've ever muttered or heard in moments of paramount frustration. Stir them together well in a vortex, along with the sight of the passenger compartment gradually taking on water at an alarming rate, and you'll get an idea of what it was like putting up the frame for the top on the car.

Then came the top itself, a piece of stitched and pleated canvas, fitted to fasten snugly to the frame by means of snapping around the body and/or on the top of the windshield, at least in theory. The canvas was not pliable, nor did it have much give for stretching. To compound the unforgiving canvas, the snaps often seemed to be just a little out of alignment. Usually, by the time you either got the canvas secured or just gave up on those last few snaps and got into the car, soaking wet and cursing, the car had taken on enough water to call for a bilge pump. Of course, by this time, too, the windshield would be misted over from the enormous amount of condensation forming in the cramped cockpit, a big

problem in the days before automatic defrosters. Crude as it was in terms of creature comforts, unless you lived in the arid Southwest, enthusiasts got used to planning drives around weather conditions if at all possible. Because what was the point of driving a roadster with the top up?

Through the 1960s, the removal and placement of the top continued to be at best an annoying chore. In *Road and Track* road tests of roadsters from the 1950s and '60s, countless paragraphs were dedicated to explaining what was required to get the top on and off. The softtop didn't become truly user friendly until toward the turn of the 1980s, when electric servomotors and precision alignment of components replaced broken fingernails and tapped patience. Until then, the process of removing the top and getting it back on was something that motorists simply had to deal with if they wanted the full roadster experience.

A Bump in the Road

In terms of production numbers, roadsters reached their zenith in the mid- to late 1960s. Enthusiasts were faced with many choices, particularly from Europe, in a variety of price ranges. From small entry-level models like the MG Midget on up to the pricey XKE Jaguars, there was a model for every wallet. But this exciting period would be dealt a crushing blow during the turbulent '70s. A global gasoline shortage, a population becoming concerned over the negative impact of the automobile on the environment, and a growing awareness of the need for increased safety-related embellishments to be built into cars came close to sounding the death knell for the roadster. It was a period of often hastily enacted U.S. government mandates that regulated everything from the height of bumpers to average fuel economy across model lines to the amount of emissions exiting the tailpipe.

European carmakers, which were not faced with the same kinds of regulations, now had to make costly adjustments to their cars in order to sell them in the lucrative U.S. market. Many European manufacturers of roadsters lacked the resources—especially the capital—to develop systems to meet these government-mandated demands. In spite of stopgap measures, some famous makers disappeared from the U.S. market during this period, among them Austin-Healey, Triumph, and, eventually, even the popular MG.

Perhaps the surest sign of the roadster's demise was the announcement by Cadillac in 1975 that it would be dropping convertibles, always popular sellers, from its product line. If Cadillac, a division of General Motors, one of the pillars of the U.S. auto industry, couldn't afford to engineer and produce a convertible to meet the new regulations, what would become of the low-volume roadsters? The outlook was bleak for the continued production of roadsters anywhere, especially if they were to be sold in the United States.

Happily, though, fine engineering and creative design prevailed and the roadster's popularity began to take hold, then increase once again during the economic boom of the mid- to late 1980s. Mercedes had always kept a roadster in its lineup, and the SL series grew in popularity as the go-go yuppies of the era looked for new and exciting ways to show off their wealth. But it was Japanese manufacturer Mazda that sensed the pent-up demand, and took the bold step to fill an up-and-coming niche with a peppy little roadster. In 1989 Mazda released the Miata, a Lotus Elan–inspired two-seater that was not only affordable but came with the added bonus of rock-solid Japanese reliability, something that had been sorely missing from the previously available European models.

The instant success of the Miata prompted manufacturers worldwide to add roadsters to their lineups for the North American market. The roadster has returned, and its reemergence is nothing short of a renaissance. Today, there is a roadster suited to just about every driver's personal style and pocketbook. Even more exciting models are on their way, solidifying the turn of the millennium as a second golden age of top-down motoring.

The history of the roadster since World War II is rich and varied; it waxes and wanes and currently is being redefined by some of the world's most famous and prestigious automakers. There have been great ones and ones that are best forgotten. There have been fast ones and those not so fast, but all have provided the driver with that unique roadster experience.

So grab your driving gloves, a light jacket, a tweed cap, and your favorite companion to share the experience. There isn't a cloud in the sky and the temperature is a perfect seventy-five degrees Fahrenheit (23.8°C). Put the top down and look for that challenging stretch of hilly and winding back road that allows you and the roadster to be as one. In sharing this experience you are part of a rich tradition that spans the better part of a century, in the United States, Europe, and beyond.

OPPOSITE: *The first roadster indigenous to the United States was the Chevrolet Corvette. Introduced in 1953, it became an icon of American automotive design and engineering almost overnight. The Corvette combined some of the handling characteristics of European sports cars with the hallmark of U.S. automotive design, a muscular V8 engine.*

LEFT: *In the late 1980s, just when it seemed the roadster was dead and buried, along came this little car from Japan. Inspired by Colin Chapman's 1960s-vintage Lotus Elan, the Mazda MX5, better known as the Miata, reinvented the roadster experience. Its success opened the way for the return of new and exciting roadsters from some of the world's premier auto makers.*

chapter ONE

THE QUINTESSENTIAL ROADSTER: MG

Okay, close your eyes and think *roadster*.
What does your imagination conjure up? For
many people—myself included—the image of a
T Series MG immediately flashes across
the wide-screen theater of the mind. Ideally, in
keeping with tradition, it should be in British
Racing Green with a rich contrasting
tan interior, although red makes a pretty
picture as well.

MG's Postwar Classic

If a single car could be selected as *the* model that epitomized the perfection of British roadster design, you'd be hard-pressed to find a more suitable candidate than the MG-TC, introduced in 1947. The shape was perfect in its time, and created the quintessential image of the postwar roadster: a tall upright grille, a slatted hood widening back to an intimate cockpit appointed in sports fittings, informative gauges, snug-fitting seats, and an abbreviated tail with the spare tire mounted tastefully on the gas tank. The fenders—which appear more suited to a bicycle than to a car—shadowed high, skinny tires on delicate wire wheels, and were hung separately at the four corners of the car, connected in the sweep under the door in a prewar stylized running board. The overall shape of the MG-TC is timeless. Place a 1947 MG-TC next to a modern BMW Z-3 and you can easily see the visionary genius that was "Morris Garage," or MG, in the mid-1940s; at the same time you can appreciate the evolution of the roadster over a fifty-year span.

The sight of a minuscule MG-TC, top down, motoring along a back road or highway in the late 1940s or early '50s must have been both startling and comical to the typical U.S. driver, stuck behind the wheel of his or her plush, rolling Detroit land barge. To a population that was collectively falling in line under the hyped Detroit belief that, when it came to automobiles, bigger was better, the MG-TC looked more like a toy than a car. Available with only right-hand drive, the car was underpowered with a mere 54 horsepower, precious little when compared to V-8 Detroit iron from the period. Zero-to-sixty times for the little MG approached the half-minute mark, but once under way the taut suspension allowed a degree of handling and control that American-made cars would not approach for decades.

Though following a TC might have been comical and even annoying at times to the average driver, imagine the latter's look of disbelief when the straightaway began to twist and wind, and the zippy TC accelerated away while our once-smug driver hammered the brakes, land-barge tires squealing in protest! Authorities from legendary race drivers to automotive journalists have insisted for years that it's more fun and challenging to drive a slow car fast than a fast car fast: to motor quickly, a slower car requires more involvement and skills on the part of the driver. They all must have had the early MG experience at some point in their careers to make such an insightful and true statement.

MG Evolution

The MG-TC was to evolve over the next decade into the TD and TF models. Bearing a strong resemblance to the TC, these later models were improved and refined versions of the TC, both performancewise and aesthetically. Out of respect for the burgeoning U.S. market, the TD and all subsequent MGs were offered with the steering wheel on the left. The popularity, performance, and affordability of the T series MGs allowed many enthusiasts the chance to go weekend racing with these cars; the Sports Car Club of America originated as an offshoot of an MG club.

PREVIOUS PAGES: *The TD established MG's reputation in the United States and set the parameters for future roadster design. Compared to the TC, it featured improved independent front suspension, wider wheels and tires, and better over-the-road performance, most noticeable on winding back roads. Since the TD was also the first MG to offer left-hand drive, most of the production run was shipped directly to the U.S.*

ABOVE: *The compact flight deck of the 1952 MG-TD Mk II exchanged creature comforts for an intimate relationship with the car itself. Once you were underway, the wind was in your face, the gearbox whined inches away from your feet, and the exhaust sang just over your shoulder.*

OPPOSITE: *From the front end, the MG-TD displayed 1930s design carried over to the 1950s, in the tall upright grille and radiator housing, separate fenders, streamlined headlight nacelles, and rudimentary straight bumper. What might have been a dated look, however, became a signature part of the T-series design.*

PAGES 18–19: *No roadster design has ever aged as gracefully as the TC. From the delicate wire wheels, raked windshield, and swoop of the fender flowing into the running board to the slatted bonnet and the spare mounted out back on the fuel tank, it compels you to slide behind the wheel.*

In 1955 MG did away with the classic, beloved prewar styling cues of separate fenders and short rear end in favor of the sleek and exciting MGA roadster. With its swept-back, streamlined rendition of the famous upright grille of the T series, the A model was an immediate success. It evolved over the next seven years but by 1962, its final year, sales were suffering, due primarily to a lack of power under the A's hood. The 1960s were to become the decade of speed, with enormous increases in horsepower, acceleration, and top-end speed—areas in which the A was sadly lacking.

POWERING UP IN THE 1960s

The demise of the underpowered A model did not spell the end for MG. On the contrary, the boys at Morris Garage began to rethink their roadster, adding a slightly bigger engine under the hood and refining design and handling as well as creature comforts. They succeeded in creating one of the most popular British roadsters ever, the MGB.

The MGB roadster was released in 1962 and was to become one of MG's most popular and sought-after roadsters. It had a production run of almost twenty years, and spawned a variety of versions including a coupe and the more powerful model C. The MGC featured an in-line six-cylinder engine, a first in the B series of MGs,

OPPOSITE: *The MGA's contours were sleek and inviting, even seductive. Its flowing lines made the marque more attractive to a wider range of buyers, a market ever more conscious of appearance.*

RIGHT, TOP: *The MGA, a radical departure from the previous T series, brought the marque into the modern era when it was introduced in 1955. The classic upright grille was reshaped but still recognizably belonged to an MG; the body was streamlined. Refined yearly, the production run ended with the 1962 1600 MK II pictured here. With discs up front, a top speed of just over 100 miles per hour (161kph), and zero-to-sixty times in the 13s, the 1600 was a fitting finale to this marvelous roadster.*

RIGHT, BOTTOM: *By 1960, the classic elements of the T series were virtually gone. Although the sloping trunk deck with optional luggage rack was less dashing than the T's classic spare on the fuel tank, and the taillight housings tended to clutter the beautiful trailing arc of the rear fender, the MGA was modern in every sense.*

which had always featured a four-cylinder powerplant beneath the bonnet. In 1973 a B model GT coupe was offered with a small-block Rover V-8 that was on a par performancewise with the premier benchmark sports car of the period, the Datsun 240-Z. Unfortunately for American drivers, the Rover-powered BGT was never available in the United States; due to its aging design, the V-8-powered car did not become a big seller in Europe and was never imported to the States.

A series of mergers and shake-ups in the late 1960s sent waves of change through the British motor industry. British Motor Corporation (BMC), owner of MG, merged with Jaguar to form British Motor Holdings (BMH). Shortly after, BMH merged with the Leyland Group to form British Leyland. When the chips fell, the group found itself with two similarly priced and competing sports car marques, MG and Triumph. There was much redundancy between similarly priced models, such as the MG Midget and the Triumph Spitfire, and the TR-6 and the MGB. While the expense of research and development of new models went to the more successful Triumph, the MGB soldiered on and, through the 1970s, continued to be produced and sold in North America and in Europe despite increasingly poor quality control and diminished performance.

But new emission and crash standards in the United States were way beyond the bleak economics of British Leyland. Instead of developing a new MG, stopgap measures were applied to the existing B. These included a de-tuning of the engine and the indignity of raising the entire suspension to meet the United States uniform-bumper-height requirement. This raising of the chassis without additional suspension modifications made the once fine-handling MG into a top-heavy, wallowing beast on any challenging road. To add insult to injury, the MGB's classic chrome grille was replaced with a one-piece black-rubber bumper/grille assembly of highly questionable aesthetics. In 1977 sway bars were added to the suspension, which returned to the model some of the fine-handling characteristics for which the Bs were known. Unfortunately the move proved to be too little, too late, and production of the MGB ceased in 1980.

THE MIDGET

MG offered yet another roadster along with the B, from 1961 on up until 1979: the Midget. The Midget was for the most part an Austin-Healey Sprite rebadged as an MG. Austin-Healey was then a division of British Motor Corporation and produced its own line of successful roadsters. Smaller and lower priced than the MGB, the Midget proved to be a popular seller in the United States and allowed many an enthusiast on a tight budget entrée into the magical realm of roadster ownership. The Midget was just that—a diminutive version of the larger B model. For a driver more than six feet (1.8m) tall it was a tight fit, and getting behind the wheel of the Midget was akin to strapping on an overcoat; once under way, you could drop your arm out the side window and literally drag your knuckles along the roadway. But this snug fit did have its advantages, as it increased the level of involvement between driver, machine, and road.

ABOVE: *The MGB, released in 1962, manifested the more square and more functional look of the 1960s, which replaced the streamlined designs of the 1950s. The upright grille had morphed into a thin, horizontal, recessed element, but the car still manifested its good bones. The B has long combined rugged reliability and traditional roadster values in a most attractive package.*

OPPOSITE: *The 1973 MG Midget Mk III. Affordable and offering driving pleasure in spades, the MG Midget's diminutive size actually enhanced the two-seater experience. Ironically, the Midget would remain in production for almost two decades, until—along with the B—it closed the chapter of the MG's presence in the United States.*

In 1974, the Midget suffered the same kinds of degrading suspension-raising and rubber bumper/grille quick-fixes that had crippled its bigger sibling, the MGB. But instead of de-tuning the already anemic Midget engine, British Leyland used the Triumph Spitfire engine in the Midget. As a result, power actually increased slightly, and for the first time in its history the Midget could show 100 mph (160kph) on the speedometer—or would, that is, if U.S. government regulations hadn't specified that no speedometers in any car should read more than 85 miles per hour (136kph). As a result of one of the more dubious, almost comical government-mandated regulations from that period, Midget owners never knew their top-end speed. Nonetheless, the Midget was a well-liked and highly affordable roadster throughout its production run, and many wonder why Leyland never developed a model to replace it when production ceased in 1979.

From the TC to the final B, MG produced some of the most successful and popular roadsters ever sold in the United States. Rock solid and reliable for the most part, MGs today are still eagerly sought after by collectors, vintage racing enthusiasts, and baby boomers who'd longed for one as a teenager but never realized the dream of ownership. Owning and restoring a vintage MGB is relatively easy and affordable, as many aftermarket manufacturers still produce most parts and components for this best-selling model. Used MGBs are still plentiful and easy on the wallet, as are the aftermarket parts.

Yes there have been faster, better-styled, and more exotic roadsters, but there is nothing quite like the experience afforded by an MG, especially the MGB. An afternoon in one will convince even the harshest of skeptics that here is the classic British sports car at its finest, a model steeped in the rich tradition of Morris Garage. Slide into the white-piped bucket seats, marvel at the functional and beautifully grouped dash layout, crank over and blip the throttle a few times to acquaint yourself with that wonderful MG exhaust note. A few miles behind the wheel is all it will take to convince you, and leave you thinking, hoping, praying: "I want one of these . . ."

THE TRIUMPHANT TRIUMPH

f MG had one real competitor in the roadster market throughout the 1950s and '60s, it was, without a doubt, the other king of British roadsters, Triumph. Gather a group of British sports car aficionados together and in no time the arguments ensuing over the merits of MG versus Triumph will rival those of any heated Ford-versus-Chevy battle in the grandstands or infield of a NASCAR event.

TRIUMPH TRIES ROADSTERS: THE TR-2 AND -3

Hoping to ride on the coattails of MG's success at home and abroad in the late 1940s, Standard-Triumph developed its first affordable roadster, the TR-2, and released the car to an excited buying public in 1953. In spite of less than stellar handling compared to the contemporary MG, the TR-2 offered 90 horsepower and a zero-to-sixty mph (96kph) figure of a respectable "hair under twelve seconds." The swooped design of the body borrowed design cues from the more expensive Jaguar XK roadsters of the period.

The TR-2 was an immediate success in the United States and, along with its successor, the TR-3, laid the foundation for Triumph's outstanding reputation for good value for dollars spent. The TR-3, released in 1955 in response to MG's new MGA, was an improved version of the TR-2. Power increased to 95 hp and, for the first time, outside door handles appeared on a Triumph roadster. (While it is certainly hard to imagine outside door handles as being "special" in this day of hands-off cell phones, cupholders, and twenty-disc CD changers, the mid-1950s were a simpler time indeed when it came to cars.) In 1956 the TR-3 had the distinction of being the first mass-produced roadster to feature front disc brakes as standard equipment.

Best remembered from the TR-2/TR-3 series of Triumphs are the TR-3A and TR-3B, which ran in production from 1957 to 1962. An evolution of the TR-3, the 3A featured the series' signature wide chrome grille. More creature comforts were added to the interior, and luggage-toting capacity was increased. Horsepower increased slightly, but there was little gain in performance due to increased weight.

In 1961 Triumph released the TR-3B, which featured the marque's first-ever synchromesh transmission. Developed for the then upcoming TR-4, the early debut of the new gearbox set something of a precedent, as Triumph became known for adding components earmarked for future models into already existing models. Whether this was done for "running" development or to milk perhaps yet one more year out of an older model remains a mystery, although this author suspects that the move was probably based on both factors, plus a bit of one-upmanship against rival MG.

ITALIAN STYLE: THE TR-4

As successful as the homegrown TR-3 series was, Triumph's next roadster, the TR-4, introduced in 1961, would be designed outside the UK by the renowned Italian designer Michelotti. Despite improved comforts, including an increase in interior space that gave taller drivers and passengers a bit of much-needed room, the TR-4 had a macho, no-nonsense style that befitted its rugged reputation. Improvements were made over the production run and, with the addition of an independent rear suspension in 1964, the TR-4 was rebadged the TR-4A.

A ROADSTER BY TWO NAMES: THE TR-5/TR-250

In 1968 Triumph replaced the standard 2.1-liter four-cylinder engine in the TR-4A with a 2.5-liter straight six. In Europe, the car was called the TR-5, continuing the traditional numerical-sequence nomenclatures of previous Triumph models. But in the United States, where drivers were head over heels in love with speed, horsepower, and exotic-sounding models such as the Pontiac GTO, Oldsmobile 4-4-2, GT-350 Mustang, and Plymouth Barracuda, the new Triumph was named the TR-250.

PREVIOUS PAGES: *Stately . . . and a little bit homely. The Triumph 1800 did offer the roadster experience, but performance was never the car's forte: its top speed was in the mid–seventy-mile-an-hour (112.6kph) range, while it made zero to sixty in the tortoise-like time of a hair over thirty seconds. Nevertheless, considering that Great Britain was rebuilding from the ravages of World War II, a ride in the country with the top down in this TR must have been heavenly.*

ABOVE: *Released in 1955, the TR-3 followed up on the success of the TR-2. Creature comforts—including outside door handles, missing on the previous model—and an increase in power were added in an attempt to give the roadster an edge against rival MG.*

OPPOSITE: *The TR-2/TR-3 Series finished up with the TR-3A. Its spotting feature was the wide chrome grille and door handles—at shin/kneecap level! Change came slowly to tradition-bound English manufacturers, but, despite being somewhat long in the tooth, the TR-3A proved to be the most popular and best seller of the series.*

With this model, the deep throaty exhaust note of the Triumph in-line six (which would be the hallmark of the later TR-6 model) was born; the distinctive bulge on the hood of the TR-250, necessary to fit the big six beneath the bonnet, is a key spotting feature for the model. The TR-250 also featured a set of racing stripes over the front of the hood between the forward wheel arches, a popular design theme on many cars from the period. Although the engine was de-tuned from its European counterpart to meet the new U.S. emission requirements, the change had no adverse effect on the popularity of the roadster in the United States. The Triumph TR-250 maintained the reputation of affordability and reliability in a fine top-down roadster for which Triumph was renowned.

TR-6: THE BEST FOR LAST

The next totally new Triumph model offered in the TR series was the stunning TR-6. If the TR-4 and the TR-250 were macho in design, the German Karmann-designed body of the TR-6 was downright ballsy. No roadster looked or sounded like the TR-6. It was low to the ground and squared off and angular at just the right places, but the crowning touches were fat red-lined radials that filled enormous wheel arches that came up nearly to the top edge of the body. The TR-6 was one of those rare cars that seemed to be moving with authority and purpose even while standing still. The TR-6 was raised slightly, far less than the MGB; nor did it suffer the enormous rubber bumper indignities heaped on the MGB. A simple set of tasteful black rubber bumper guards front and rear allowed the TR-6 to meet U.S. regulations.

Nonetheless, 1976 marked the end of the TR-6, as Triumph prepared a new sports car, the TR-7. (Early on during my run up the learning curve of cars foreign, I thought there was nothing more desirable than a British Racing Green TR-6. While attending college I took a job as a car polisher at a Triumph/SAAB dealer on Staten Island just to be near one.)

TRIUMPH'S LITTLE SPITFIRE

To compete with the Austin-Healey Sprite and MG Midget roadster, Triumph in 1962 released the Spitfire Mk 1. The carmaker had turned once again to Michelotti, and the Spitfire was an immediate success, due in no small part to its sleek Italian design. The entire hood of the Spitfire was hinged at the forward edge and made any routine or major maintenance an easy task. The "Spit," as it came to be known among the Triumph cognoscenti, was faster than the Sprites or Midgets of the period and featured front disc brakes. It enjoyed respectable sales and popularity in North America during

OPPOSITE: *By 1974, the Triumph Spitfire was hamstrung by the impact of U.S. government regulations. The hideous rubber "battering rams" on the bumpers marred the roadster's fine and delicate lines, while, under the full-tilt bonnet, the engine had been strangled to meet emission standards. Top speed was a paltry 80 mph (128.7kph), and zero-to-sixty times were in VW Beetle company, close to sixteen seconds. The top did go down, though, so its roadster appeal kept the Spitfire going.*

RIGHT: *With German styling wrapped around TR-250 underpinnings, the TR-6 offered decent performance in a most attractive body. The macho stance and appearance of this 1973 model are enhanced by the chin-spoiler and Hella driving lights. The following year, however, the TR began its slide into oblivion: the powers-that-were raised the suspension and added rubber bumper guards, and the engine lost still more horsepower—all in the name of meeting U.S. regulations.*

its formidable eighteen-year production run. Like its competitors, the Sprite and Midget, the Spitfire offered lots of bang for the buck—great style at an affordable price—and was an ideal model for entry-level roadster buyers.

THE STAG

Triumph's fortunes began to wane in North America in the mid-1970s. Parent company British Leyland was in serious trouble, suffering from a lack of cash for developing new models, mismanagement at all levels, and poor quality control in the factories that were still operating after the mergers. The car that illustrated these problems was the Stag.

Introduced in 1970, the Stag was Triumph's entry into the burgeoning high-end GT market. While not a true roadster (as it offered two-plus-two seating), the Stag was more luxurious in interior appointments and featured a V-8, with marked increased performance over the TR-6. From the outset—largely because of Triumph's

insistence on rushing the car to market before it was fully developed—the car suffered from dismally poor quality control and serious reliability problems, most notably in the cooling system. Blown head gaskets were a common and expensive repair as a result of this serious shortcoming.

Poor engineering decisions made early on in the Stag's development led to the car's early demise in the North American market. Instead of dropping a tried and proven Rover V-8 into this model, Leyland elected to create a hybrid V-8 by joining two slant four engines from a European-only model, the Triumph Dolomite sedan. However, a lack of capital prevented the proper development of this new engine.

If one car reflected the eventual decline of the British motor industry at that point in history, it was the Stag. It was not unusual for dealers to have to painstakingly go over the entire car and correct simple and sloppy manufacturing defects like loose bolts on half shafts, miswired radios, and headlights that wouldn't

dim due to faulty high-beam switches. This author knows from experience that it was not unusual for an excited new owner to take delivery of his Stag and drive off, only to return a few hours later with a laundry list of defects that had become painfully apparent in but a few short hours of frustrating ownership. Worse yet were the owners who returned riding shotgun in the front seat of a tow truck with their disabled Stag hanging dead on the hook. The troublesome and ill-fated Stag foreshadowed the declining fortunes of the once proud Triumph name.

THE TR-7

Beginning in 1975, following the TR-6 in production, was Triumph's first all-new two-seat car in over a decade, the TR-7. Breaking with the styling tradition of the squared-off macho shapes of the TR-4, TR-4A, TR-250, and the successful TR-6, Triumph went to a wedge shape. Oddly, Triumph initially offered the car as a hardtop only. Perhaps this was an indication that, in spite of their long history of roadster production, Triumph sensed that the buying climate of the mid- to late 1970s was veering away from two-seat convertibles. It wasn't until four years later that Triumph realized it had made a huge blunder in not offering the TR-7 as a roadster.

When the roadster model was finally released in 1979, it was way too little, way too late for Triumph. Their once solid reputation for building rugged and reliable cars had been seriously eroded by reliability problems and poor quality control over the first four years of the TR-7's production run.

THE TR-8: THE END OF THE LINE

In 1980, as yet another stopgap measure, Triumph dropped a small-block Rover V-8 into the TR-7's engine bay and labeled the car (naturally) the TR-8. It was indeed a dark hour for British Leyland; relying on tradition and a dulled, fast-fading reputation, the powers-that-be chose to cross-pollinate car lines with a variety of engine and component swaps without doing any real new engineering on the cars. Meanwhile, an increasingly savvy buying public was beginning to embrace the high level of quality control and engineering found in Japanese cars. British cars, particularly sports cars like Triumph, were now seen as potential nightmares to own as their reputation for poor quality and low reliability spread.

Had Triumph released the TR-8 instead of the TR-7 back in 1975, and given it a more refined suspension and suitable, beefed-up brakes to accommodate the increase in weight brought on by the V-8, Triumph's downward spiral might have been arrested. Yet another legendary marque and maker of some of the best affordable roadsters ever to be sold in North America vanished forever from the landscape in 1981.

Faulty management and horrible marketing and engineering decisions at British Leyland proved to be the final blow for the beloved Triumph, yet the Triumph name still rings magically in any discussion of fine roadsters. Their rugged nature and affordability on the used-car market ensures that Triumphs will remain in demand, and that many will still be running for years to come.

OPPOSITE: *Sleek and well-styled, it's no wonder the Spitfire outsold its rivals, the cost-competitive Austin-Healey Sprite and MG Midget. The otherwise well-balanced design of the 1967 Mk III was compromised by a front bumper mounted high and in the middle of the grille, only the first of many hasty changes made to Triumphs bound for the United States.*

TOP: *The TR-4 brought the boxy Michelotti style that gave Triumph its macho image; here embodied in the 1967 TR4A.*

ABOVE: *Though stylish, the 1977 Triumph Stag suffered from an unreliable hybrid engine that fueled the marque's reputation for poor workmanship.*

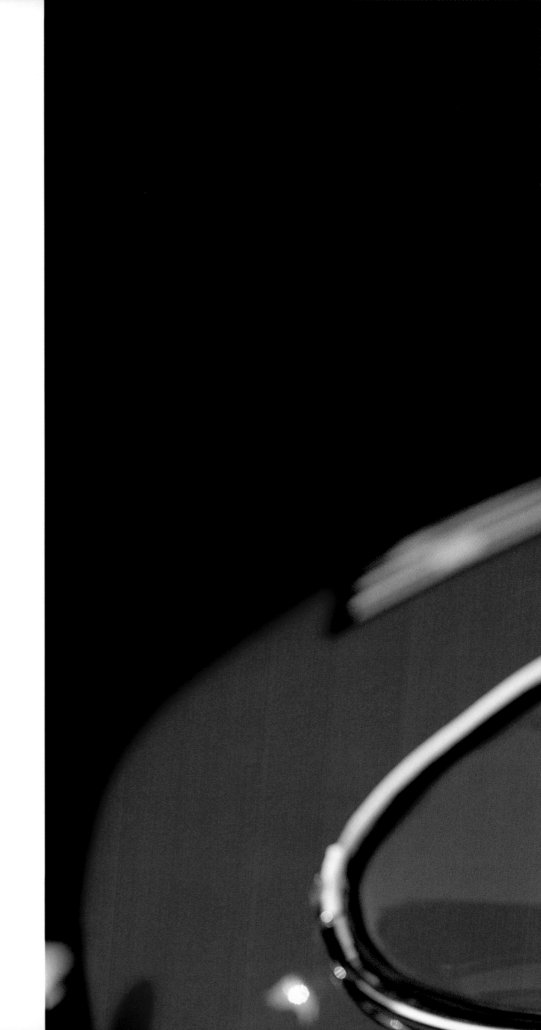

chapter THREE

OTHER BRITISH CLASSICS

While MG and Triumph may have dominated the market, there were a few other great British carmakers turning out classic roadsters during the postwar era as well. Along with MG and Triumph, they set the standard for outdoor motoring, and classics from Jaguar, Lotus, Austin-Healey, and Morgan continue to influence roadster design today.

JAGUAR

The term "legendary" may be rightly applied to the British sports car Jaguar. Founded in the 1920s by William Lyon, the firm, originally

called the Swallow Sidecar Company, built sidecars for motorcycles. In the late 1920s, Swallow began to produce custom bodies for the popular Austin Seven automobile. The custom body business grew, and eventually the firm began to produce their own cars. In 1935 Swallow produced its first true two-seat roadster, and the next year it introduced the great SS-100—along with the first use of the "Jaguar" name. The firm grew steadily until automobile production ceased for the duration of World War II.

THE JAG IS BORN: THE XK-120

Despite the near total destruction of Coventry, Jaguar's home base, the factory emerged from the war relatively unscathed and set about building a succession of roadsters that today are stars in the roadster firmament. First off the assembly line in 1948 was the XK-120, which defined Jaguar for all models to come. It is interesting to note that the XK-120 was almost an afterthought—the car was supposed to be a sedan, the Mk VII saloon. Development of the sedan took longer than expected, and so a two-seat roadster body was placed on a shortened sedan chassis. The XK-120 was an immediate success, to the surprise and delight of Jaguar; this "afterthought" would determine the company's direction for decades to come.

The XK-120's dual overhead cam straight six produced a booming 160 horsepower, yielded a zero-to-sixty figure of under ten seconds, and a top end of more than 120 miles per hour (190kph). In its time few cars, let alone a roadster,

PREVIOUS PAGES: *There's no mistaking the XKE, even in an almost abstract detail photograph.*

ABOVE LEFT: *It is easy to appreciate the brilliance of Jaguar design in this stunning 1955 XK-140 SE. From any angle, in any light, the car is as close to perfection as any car of its time.*

LEFT: *Jaguar introduced the XK-150, last of the 120/140 series, in 1957. Four-wheel disc brakes were an innovation, but the mystique was never quite there.*

OPPOSITE: *When it was introduced in 1947, the XK-120 was the fastest car in its price range. Unprepared for the XK-120's immediate success, Jaguar had to scramble to meet the surprising demand.*

PAGES 36-37: *The front end of the 1938 Jaguar SS-100 combines grace and incredible performance—this legendary roadster, the first to carry the Jaguar name, set a standard for both that would guide the marque into the postwar years.*

offered such stellar performance. Even so, the XK-120's best-selling feature was its stunning shape. Nothing like it had ever been seen before. So beautiful and seductive was the look of this car that eager buyers were more than happy to accept cramped seating and limited luggage-carrying capacity. The XK-120 was followed, in 1954, by the further-refined XK-140. The engine moved forward for more interior space, horsepower was increased to 190, and a coupe version was offered for the first time.

TAKING IT TO THE TRACK

Jaguar realized the significance of racing and winning on the track to promoting and selling its line of high-performance cars early on in the game. In 1951 Jaguar developed the C Type race car from the XK-120 platform. Upgraded with a more

refined suspension, better brakes, a strengthened frame, a new, more aerodynamic body, plus a tweaked engine pumping out 210 horsepower, Jaguar scored its first win at the prestigious 24 Hours of Le Mans in 1951.

With the C Type's successor, the D Type, Jaguar would go on to four more victories at Le Mans, in 1953, '55, '56, and '57. Involvement in a disastrous, controversial accident in 1955 tarnished their win that year. A Jaguar was involved in an accident with a Mercedes and the ensuing wreckage—including the engine of the Mercedes—scythed through the crowd, killing more than eighty spectators. Jaguar had no wins in '56, and at the end of that year withdrew their factory effort. Jaguar did, however, support the Scottish team, Ecurie Ecosse, which won the race with a Jaguar in 1957.

In 1957 Jaguar built a small series of lightweight roadsters for the road, the XKSS, using the surplus D Type components it had on hand. It was, out of the box,

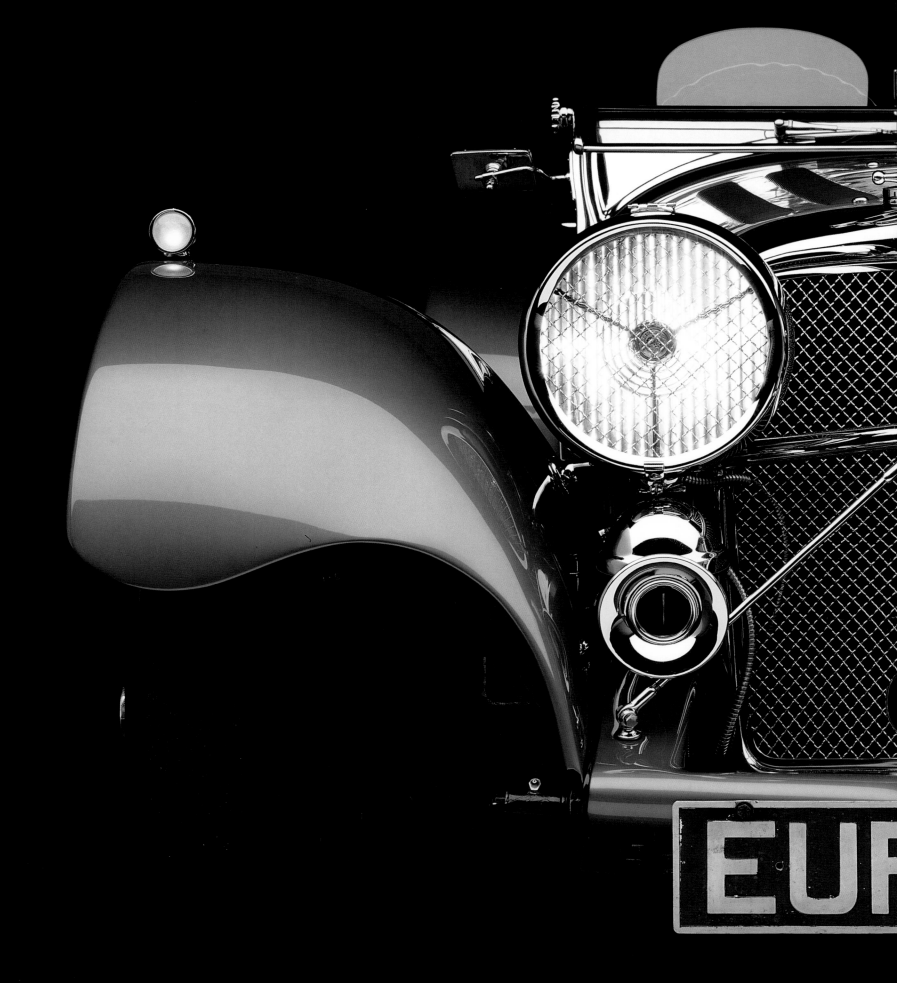

THIS PAGE: *Built with surplus D Type racing components, this 1957 XKSS roadster was the civilized, road-going version of the D Type Le Mans–winning race car—if you consider 265 hp civilized! What Jaguar's fortunes might have been had this car been produced in any great numbers is open to speculation: a fire destroyed the factory after only sixteen examples had been built. In 1964, however, out of the ashes of the XKSS would rise the legendary XK E Type.*

OPPOSITE: *The elegant front end of the 1962 XKSS E Type displays glass covers over the headlight—the finishing touch to its fine, flowing lines.*

the best-handling car of its day. Lightweight, with brakes and horsepower to match, its production, however, was halted in 1957 by a fire at the factory.

THE XKE: JAG'S CLASSIC ROADSTER

In 1961 Jaguar introduced what was to become the car most associated with the company: the XKE roadster. Like the short-lived XKSS, the XKE was a refined road version of the D Type. It featured an independent rear axle, the first for Jaguar. Engine output was a whopping 265 horsepower from a 3.8-liter in-line dual overhead cam six. As they were with the XK-120, buyers of the XKE were so taken aback by the drop-dead-gorgeous design and style, they cared little that the cockpit was cramped, that there was little luggage-carrying capacity, or that the engine had a healthy, almost voracious appetite for oil. The car was an immediate success.

From 1965 to '71 the E Type went through an evolutionary process of refinements, sometimes countermanded by the effects of the times. The engine grew to 4.2 liters, although its performance was dampened by the new U.S. emission requirements; top speed was still a respectable 125 miles per hour (200kph) in the "Americanized" engine. Both a coupe and a rather ungainly shaped and elongated two-plus-two were offered along with the roadster.

In 1971 Jaguar took the lengthened chassis from the two-plus-two coupe and dropped a V-12 engine under the bonnet to restore the high-level performance that had long been its hallmark. The exquisite, almost perfectly proportioned shape of the XKE roadster was lost in this newest incarnation. The new V-12 model did show its descent from the perfectly proportioned XKE, but at the expense of adding a long snoot to accommodate the V-12 and a wide midsection for increased interior space. In deference to the U.S. market and the emerging "luxury" car segment of the market, the new E Type Series III V-12 offered such amenities as power steering and an automatic transmission as options.

Although Jaguar had always been an expensive car, as opposed to the bread-and-butter, affordable roadsters offered by MG and Triumph, the new V-12 pushed Jaguar into a higher price range than that in which it had previously existed and prospered. The roadster did not sit well in this higher-end market, and by 1975 the E Type was dropped, ending roadster production. Jaguar concentrated its efforts on the stunning and successful XJ series of sedans, and continued to produce sedans through the 1980s, although it soon became apparent to management that Jaguar lacked the resources to develop new cars, particularly for the United States, its most lucrative market.

Jaguar entered into merger talks with General Motors, but, taken over in 1989 by Ford in a hostile bid, fell under the umbrella of old Henry's formidable "Blue Oval." Jaguar remained independent within Ford and introduced a new roadster to take advantage of the growing market for roadsters in the 1990s.

LEFT: *This 1999 Jaguar XK8 roadster picks up where the XKE left off, that is, after production of the E Type Series III stopped in 1975. While styling cues such as the oval front intake opening and the hood's contours are unmistakable carryovers from the E Type, the XK8 achieves more high-end luxury than even the twelve-cylinder E Types. Built for a different market, it nonetheless maintains the rich Jaguar tradition of performance and style.*

OPPOSITE: *What price a twelve-cylinder engine and more creature comforts? Elongated and slightly bulbous in the midsection, this 1973 Series III was the last of the production run of the XK E Type. While it performed better than the previous six-cylinder XKEs, you may judge whether the design is equal to, let alone an improvement over, the stunning Series I and II.*

LOTUS

In his time, there was no individual in the automotive field more innovative, daring, and consistently able to think and engineer outside the box than Lotus founder Colin Chapman. Chapman's forte was racing, first with sports racers and later with much success and many championships in Formula One—in fact, Chapman defined Formula One with his startling engineering innovations.

Chapman's roadster creations, like his race cars, were designed with a simple formula based on performance first and foremost: build the car as light as possible, and give it the finest-handling suspension (one pioneered by Chapman). The need for a high-horsepower engine was not all that important—most of Chapman's more notable creations were powered by a simple and rugged four-cylinder double overhead-cam Coventry Climax engine that produced power in the somewhat meager 100-plus horsepower range. Sedate, it would seem, in light V-8 engines, but the combination of Chapman's creative suspension design and the balanced, light weight of the car combined to provide a driving experience second to none when the road became twisty and winding.

THE LOTUS SEVEN

Lotus produced a series of roadsters in the 1950s and early '60s that were primarily designed for racing. One car, the Seven Series, or Lotus Seven, was a roadgoing

adaptation of the Lotus sports racers of the time. Production began in 1957 and the design was the embodiment of all that was Chapman. The car was offered in kit form to take advantage of loopholes in the British tax exemptions, and its no-nonsense design was often referred to in the press and among enthusiasts as a "motorcycle on four wheels." It was in essence a bare-bones roadster designed for maximum performance. Spartan in terms of creature appointments or comforts, the small fiberglass roadster was made simply to go as fast as possible within the horsepower parameters of the engine.

Not a car for everyday use, the Seven became, however, the standard-bearer for enthusiasts who dreamed of racing but lacked the resources needed to seriously pursue the sport. For those lucky and talented enough to race, it offered a competitive package at an attractive price, and a legion of fellow owners on the track to compete with. So popular was the Lotus Seven that today the same car is being produced, albeit with larger engines and refined suspensions, plus a few creature comforts, by Caterham in England. It is still a roadster much sought after by those who know of its attributes and appreciate and desire its Chapman lineage.

THE LOTUS ELAN

The production car (and true roadster) that put Lotus on the map, though, was the Lotus Elan S1. Prior to the Elan, Lotus had produced the Elite, a less than successful

LEFT: *Early on, Lotus designed cars strictly for racing—this 1957 Lotus 11 Club, one of the first, would spawn the first of the infamous Seven series roadsters, the Series One. Chapman's and Lotus's innovation and success in Formula One would set standards in the sport for decades. Renowned drivers, with names like Clark, Rindt, Hill, Fittipaldi, Peterson, and Senna, would forever be linked to the marque.*

OPPOSITE: *Colin Chapman's first production car, the Lotus Mk VI was engineered and built for a variety of racing conditions, including hills, roads, and trials. It came with a choice of engines: either a Ford or an MG four-cylinder. When combined with Chapman's brilliant suspension design, the car's performance belied its modest horsepower.*

THIS PAGE: *To many Lotus enthusiasts the Elan S4 Sprint is the most desirable of all Elan models, because of the engine's increased horsepower and a noticeable improvement in quality and reliability. Finished in the two-tone colors of Gold Leaf Tobacco, then sponsor of Lotus Formula One, this 1963 Elan is typical of the breed. Look carefully at the S4, as a certain Japanese automaker did, ensuring that the roadster will be around for generations to come.*

OPPOSITE: *After the demise of the Elan in 1973, Lotus didn't offer a new Elan—or any roadster for that matter— until 1989. This 1991 Elan shows its lineage, but under the hood lurked controversy: the new model had front-wheel drive and was powered by an Isuzu engine. It was a product of the global auto industry: GM now owned Lotus and a big chunk of Isuzu. Like its predecessor, though, the new Elan provided incredible handling and performance in a small package.*

hardtop two-seater. Although the Elite's fiberglass monocoque design was quite innovative, the car suffered dismally from poor build quality and iffy reliability. On the verge of bankruptcy in 1962, Lotus launched the Elan, a more mainstream design than the somewhat eccentric Elite. A steel backbone frame replaced the troublesome monocoque, and the signature Chapman-designed suspension hung on each corner of the frame. A simple but elegant fiberglass body was mated to the frame, and in spite of occasional shoddy build problems the car was a smashing success for Lotus.

The Elan remained in production through various upgrades, ending with the best incarnation of the lineage, the Elan S4, introduced in 1968. By '68 Lotus had greatly improved its quality, though reliability was still questionable, and the later models became the most desirable of all the Elans. The Elan S4 Sprint, released in a stunning two-tone red-and-white paint job that mirrored the Gold Leaf Tobacco–sponsored Lotus 72 Formula One cars of the time, was the best-performing Elan. The best Sprints, those rare examples fitted with a five-speed gearbox, were capable of 125 miles per hour (200kph) top speed and a zero-to-sixty time of 6.8 seconds. More than respectable indeed for an engine of this modest size.

It was the fine handling characteristics of the Elan that made them highly desirable among enthusiasts—then as well as today—as classic roadsters. How truly fine and special a road car the Elan was may best be seen and appreciated in the Mazda Miata of today. The Mazda Miata might be called the cornerstone of the rebirth of the roadster in the late 1980s: small, lightweight, great performance, all at an affordable price. Sound familiar? When Mazda set out to redefine and build a true roadster for the 1990s, the Lotus Elan was chosen as *the* car to emulate. Place a Miata side by side with an Elan and the similarities are astounding, but it was Lotus and Colin Chapman who had set the standard that defined the roadster some thirty years previously.

THE ELAN RETURNS: A LOTUS REVIVAL

Colin Chapman died in 1982 and Lotus was bought by British Car Auctions. In 1986, this company, on the verge of bankruptcy, sold Lotus to General Motors, which controls the company to this day.

A new Elan was offered in 1989, the SE. Breaking with tradition, the Elan SE was powered through the front wheels, a shock to true roadster enthusiasts who cherished the sheer thrill of sliding the tail out and powering through a turn, which could be provided only by rear wheel drive. But the Elan SE handled as magnificently as any Lotus that had preceded it.

ABOVE: *From the front this 1996 Lotus Elise is the picture of raw motoring pleasure. The opening down low looks an awful lot like the opening on the old Elan S series—a very nice tribute to the past in such a futuristic automobile.*

OPPOSITE: *Present-day print ads for the Lotus Esprit claim that it's a car that would make the late Colin Chapman smile. If that's the case, this 1999 Elise would make him smile till it hurt. The Elise embodies everything that Chapman felt a sports car was all about: light weight, a small but high-performing engine, and a new standard in handling.*

Another break from tradition came in the form of a Japanese-based Isuzu twin-cam engine providing power for the new Elan. By using an in-house engine from Isuzu (also owned by GM), the company managed to revive the Elan while saving on the expensive research and design that would have been required for a new Lotus-derived power plant.

Today Lotus builds one of the most exciting and best-performing roadsters in the world, the wildly exciting Elise. In the tradition set down by Chapman, this car returned to the roots that made Lotus famous: its lightweight, fine handling, and high-performance engine. It is truly unfortunate that this incredible car is not for sale in the United States at present, although plans are afoot to bring it to American shores. For this author, the Elise has a place of honor on my list of the top three most desirable roadsters available today. While I haven't driven one, the written road tests in the automotive press in both North America and Europe have been spectacular!

AUSTIN-HEALEY

Another famous English maker of roadsters born in the postwar period is Austin-Healey, which produced a fine line of some of the most attractively styled roadsters to come out of Great Britain. The company was formed out of a merger of the Donald Healey Motor Company and Austin under the tutelage of Sir Leonard Lord, at the time with BMC.

Having seen Healey's prototype roadster at the London Auto Show of 1952, Lord became so enamored of it that he tried to interest BMC in producing the car. But BMC at that time had all their eggs in the Triumph TR-2 basket, and saw no need for a similar roadster. Lord left BMC to create the merger and from it grew a series of desirable roadsters that soon gathered a passionate and loyal following.

THE AUSTIN-HEALEY 100s

If ever an automobile was produced to go with a tweed cap, driving gloves, and ascot, it was the Austin-Healey roadster, from the 100 up to the Series 3000. The first roadster the new carmaker offered was the 100/4 in 1953. Those early 100s lacked any real engineering breakthroughs; they used stock Austin A-90 sedan components, including the chassis and engine. But the car's big selling point was its strikingly beautiful design: it was one of the finest of the time and remains so to this day. It was very affordable, while providing performance that was more than acceptable for a car in its price range. The 100, an immediate hit in the United States, became a much sought-after roadster.

A small production run of 100M models with more power was made, beginning in 1955. The 100M's design points, including a sleek, raked, narrow windshield and a two-tone paint job, were intended to imply a sense of racing or rallying. The 100M's suspension was lower than the 100/4's; although it gave the car the desired "racing" look, it often caused clearance problems on poor roads.

In 1955 a very limited number of 100S models were produced. The 100S featured front and rear disc brakes, an industry first, and weight-saving aluminum body panels. Spotting features of this rare breed were louvers on the hood and classic leather straps that held the bonnet in place. An elliptical grille replaced the original, more stately grille of the 100/4. Straight-line acceleration was the 100S's strong suit, but when the road began to twist and turn and get challenging, the weight of the Healey required strong arms on the wheel.

The year 1956 saw the introduction of the 100/6, which featured a six-cylinder engine and more interior space. An increase in horsepower was a wash, however, as the additional weight negated the gain. A revised version of the 100/6 released in the late stages of its production run improved performance somewhat.

OPPOSITE: *The Austin Healey 100/4 could do zero to sixty in a respectable 10½ seconds; it also had one of the most beautifully designed bodies of any mass-produced roadster.*

ABOVE: *Despite its six-cylinder engine, this 1958 Austin Healey 100/6 did not perform much better than the previous 100/4 four-cylinder models. The increase in power was offset by greater weight, due to more creature comforts. Nonetheless, the Austin-Healey, particularly the 100/6 in two-tone paint, was one of the finest-looking roadsters of its time.*

THE BIG 3000

In 1959 the Austin-Healey 3000 was introduced, with a 3-liter six-cylinder that pumped out a respectable 124 horsepower. Front disc brakes were offered as standard equipment—rather late for a company that was the first to put discs at all four corners on the limited-production 100S. The 3000 might not be referred to technically as a true roadster, as it featured a "quasi" rear or jump seat in back of the front buckets. How an adult would fit into that seat remains a mystery, but it did allow a bit of increased cargo- or luggage-carrying capacity. The 3000 soldiered on with small improvements each year over its nine-year production run. As in the case of other English roadster marques, however, the expense required to bring the 3000 up to the safety and engine-emission requirements of the all-important and lucrative U.S. market sealed the fate of the 3000.

The "big" Healey roadsters, the 100s through the 3000, never handled well because of their weight. Yet side by side with similarly priced roadsters throughout that period from MG and Triumph, there was no contest as to who won out in the design department. The big Healeys were stunning in their time; to encounter one on the road today is an increasingly rare visual treat to be savored.

ABOVE: *The Healey 3000 was the final evolution of the design that went back to the 100/4 of 1953. Viewed broadside, this 1960 Mark I exhibits the big Healey's strongest point: its stunning design. The two-tone paint accentuates the fine lines common to all the big Healeys.*

RIGHT: *The elegant 3000 underwent few visible changes over its decade-long production run from 1959 to 1968. This Concours condition 1965 Mk 3 is resplendent in metallic blue, offset with a striking red leather interior.*

OPPOSITE: *The interior of this 1964 Healey 3000 Mk III is classic British roadster interior at its finest. The burled wood dash, with its Jaeger gauges in logical sequence; the finely stitched seats; and the high tunnel over the drive line, the short gear lever falling magically into the hand, are all beautiful, driver-friendly, or both. Less so, especially on long hauls, is that enormous steering wheel, which always seems too close to your chest. But top-down, who's to complain?*

THE SPRITE MAKES A SPLASH

Austin-Healey's roadster legend didn't begin and end with the 100 series. Perhaps more than any other roadster, its "Frogeye" Sprite won the hearts of young and old alike. Introduced in 1958, the tiny, moderately powered Sprite fit in as a perfect complement to the company's larger roadsters. With its smiling grille and wide-eyed headlights, the Sprite seemed equally at home darting along a misty backcountry English road or in a lead role in a Disney animated feature. Though only produced for a brief three-year period, the Frogeye (it came to be known in the United States as the "Bugeye") is the Healey most remember when this beloved marque is discussed.

Performance was not its strong suit; affordability and a low-end market niche were its hallmarks. Borrowing most mechanicals from the anemic Austin A 35 "family" sedan, the Sprite was the type of car that one could toss with abandon into a turn, mash down the accelerator to awaken the 43 horsepower, and exit the turn with a smile that rivaled the steel and chrome grin on the front of the car. Of course you weren't motoring fast by any stretch of the imagination, but the sensation of almost sitting on the road, the top down and the sky above, made speed secondary. The Sprite was fun squared, a blast to drive, and it rarely bit you in return should you err. To keep costs down, the car was built with a trunk that didn't open and no external door handles. Yet it created a niche for well-priced, entry-level roadsters that all subsequent Sprite models occupied virtually alone for most of the production run.

In 1961 the Sprite was redesigned; gone, sadly, was the signature look of the frogeye. Still handsome, the new Sprite II featured front disc brakes and an optional hardtop. The Sprite was rebadged into the MG Midget during this run, and the Midget, essentially the same car as the Sprite, consistently outsold the Sprite, most likely due to the appealing aura of the MG name. In 1964 the Sprite was further improved and entered the "serious" car realm with the addition of roll-down windows and external door handles. In 1971, much to the chagrin of Austin-Healey enthusiasts, the automaker dropped the Sprite (known as the Sprite IV and Austin Sprite in its last year) from its lineup. Like the big Healeys, the Sprite was hobbled by changes in the worldwide market, and British Leyland lacked the capital to improve and engineer a new engine for the environmentally conscious U.S. market.

Through 1977, the Sprite survived in the United States as the winded and de-tuned MG Midget. In spite of its rather lackluster performance (many contemporary economy sedans would routinely blow its doors off), it did offer the top-down, wind-in-your-face roadster experience at the most affordable price.

LEFT: *With looks that place it squarely in the league of the VW Beetle—in a word, endearing—the Austin-Healey Sprite I was an immediate success. Whether called the Bugeye (Stateside), or the Frogeye (across the Pond), it offered the roadster experience at a very low price.*

OPPOSITE: *Always a roadster with impeccable looks, the 3000 Mark III carried that Healey tradition to the end of its production run in 1968.*

ABOVE: *Behold the first Morgan to sport four wheels, the 1936 Coventry Climax–powered 4/4. Before the 4/4, Morgan produced three-wheel cars—or were they motorcycles?—that were both popular, inexpensive transportation and fun to race on weekends.*

LEFT: *The Morgan 4/4 nameplate, firmly fastened to the radiator screen, was a handsome detail indeed.*

OPPOSITE: *It would have been hard to believe in 1936 that the design of that year's 4/4 would endure for sixty years, incorporating changes while retaining its signature look. Hats off to the glorious British tradition: Morgan still defines it best!*

MORGAN

The story of Morgan is steeped in tradition. No British car manufacturer has managed to produce virtually the same model automobile from 1946 to the present . . . except Morgan. The company may be considered the quintessence of the quaint English "cottage industry," except instead of jam cupboards or fine needlepoint, they're producing an automobile.

Prior to World War II, Morgan produced three-wheeled automobiles powered by motorcycle engines. Odd but cheap, reliable, and a blast to drive, the brand sparked fierce loyalty among a growing population of Morgan owners and enthusiasts. In 1936 Morgan introduced a roadster with four wheels, the 4/4, and then, with the cessation of hostilities, offered the car again starting in 1946. Possessing suspension components whose design dated to 1910, the Morgan was nevertheless well received. With a standard engine, the 4/4 became the Plus Four and was sold from 1951 through 1955. Though meager on power—the four-cylinder engine pumped out only a paltry 68 horsepower—the car was still quicker than the MG-TC.

In 1954 Morgan entered into an agreement with Triumph, and the TR-2 engine became a fixture under the hood of the Morgan for the next fifteen years, though the body remained virtually unchanged. Now, that's tradition. A small number of Morgans produced between 1955 and 1961 had Ford engines; these Ford-powered Morgans, badged 4/4 Series II and III, were horribly underpowered, with a paltry 36 horsepower fed to the wheels through an equally tortoiselike three-speed gearbox.

From 1962 through '68 the body style, relatively unchanged since the 1930s, was revised slightly to make the car a bit wider. Disc brakes appeared, along with a more powerful Ford four-banger pumping out 60 horsepower. This increase in power gave the lightweight Morgan respectable zero-to-sixty times under eleven seconds and a top end slightly more than 90 miles per hour (145kph) with a good tail wind. Suspension remained unchanged and, as with Morgan owners thirty years earlier, Morgan tradition forced new owners to suffer discomforts—such as a steering wheel that pressed into your chest if you were anything other than slight in build and bone-jarring rides. Morgan owners didn't care; being able to buy a "classic" new car kept them loyal and happy.

From 1967 through 1988 the car remained just as it had been except for the 1600/Plus Four, which came with a Ford 1600-cc four-cylinder 74-horsepower engine, the same engine, highly modified of course, that appeared in Formula Ford race cars. Morgan offered lightweight aluminum bodies on special orders to save weight and increase performance. In 1988 the Rover 2-liter dual overhead-cam four was available, and the car reverted to the old "Plus 4" name. This engine gave the Morgan power—some 138 horsepower—and yielded rather stunning performance in a car that was over the half-century mark in terms of its basic design. Zero to sixty was reached in a hair over seven and a half seconds. The harsh ride and cramped cockpit remained as always.

The Plus Eight arrived in 1968 with a small-block Rover 3.5-liter V-8 stuffed under the bonnet. The biggest changes in the body were two more inches (5cm) in length, a dashboard detail revamp, and alloy wheels. This version of the Morgan remains available as of this writing.

Morgan is a unique manufacturer, indeed, and in today's automotive market it might be called an aberration. To the faithful, there is no finer car. Handmade, like every Morgan that has preceded it, this classic roadster remains a throwback to a bygone era, with its running boards, headlight nacelles, squared-off tail, and regally upright chrome grille. Nothing else on the road can trace its origin directly back to 1936, and that uninterrupted lineage is perhaps the most appealing aspect of Morgan ownership. To be able to step way back in time to the early days of the roadster each time you slide behind the wheel is the mark of Morgan's incredibly long-lived legacy and success.

LEFT: *Why, yes, it is more streamlined than the 4/4, but this is the 1999 Morgan Plus 8, some sixty-three years newer than the original. If it is the classic British roadster experience you want, then Morgan has the car for you!*

OPPOSITE: *Some ten years older than the 1999, this 1988 Plus 8 will also get you from zero to sixty in a respectable 6.5 seconds. Why fix it if it ain't broke?*

chapter **FOUR**

AMERICAN ROADSTERS

One of the inventions that forever changed mankind during the course of the twentieth century is the automobile, and that was nowhere more apparent anywhere in the world than in the United States. Between 1920 and 1940, the automobile went from being a rich-boy's toy to a fairly common household item for most Americans. Think of the despair Americans faced when, after years of prosperity and the budding popularity of automobiles, the Great Depression put cars suddenly out of reach. Think, too, of the frustration of those same Americans when, less than fifteen years later,

PREVIOUS PAGES: *Aggressive, even mean, and unmistakable, that's the front of the 1958 Corvette—and any Corvette from 1958 to 1962.*

ABOVE: *While later designs had much more macho appeal, the first Corvette had genuine sports car distinction. This classic 1953 in Polo White, the only color available in that first year, with Sportsman Red interior and subtle red highlights, showcases the fine lines from the creative minds of Harley Earl's styling team at GM.*

OPPOSITE: *It was flashy, albeit in a non-original factory color, but the 1954 Corvette was little changed from the 1953 model. Longer exhaust tips, the small fins on the taillight housings, and the side trim molding foreshadowed the aircraft-inspired design themes that would proliferate throughout the auto industry in the jet-age fifties.*

World War II put a stop to the production of new automobiles, and strictly rationed automobile-related necessities like tires and gasoline. For a country that had passionately embraced the automobile in the 1920s and '30s, deprivation of personal mobility came as a painful shock.

By the time the war had ended and car production began again in 1946, the United States was entering an era of unprecedented prosperity, and Americans were hungry for new cars. American automakers responded in spades. Although in the years immediately following World War II the new autos being released were merely rehashes of prewar designs, within a few years American carmakers—from small independents to Detroit's Big Three—were offering new designs and bold new models. Although roadsters were rare at first, those funny little sports cars from Europe were attracting a lot of attention from customers—especially returning vets—and manufacturers. Americans were eager to get behind the wheel of an American roadster, and many automakers were ready to put them there.

AMERICA'S ROADSTER: THE CHEVROLET CORVETTE

Got a month or so? It would take that long, if not longer, to describe fully and explain best the legendary status that the Corvette has achieved in the United States. As the only true U.S. sports car, the Corvette has earned a cult following, with numerous magazines dedicated exclusively to the marque and countless loyalists devoted to specific model years.

Very, very few U.S. automobiles have been able to generate such a loyal and passionate following. Only at the Porsche Museum in Stuttgart, Germany, does one see the kind of devotion to a sports car that Corvette fans display at the Corvette Museum in Bowling Green, Kentucky—both museums beckon enthusiasts for automotive pilgrimages to the cities where their beloved cars are assembled. To wide-eyed seven-year-olds and wistful seventy-year-olds alike, the Corvette is an icon, and owning one is a mark of personal achievement. As Mike Yaeger of Mid-America Designs, one of the largest Corvette specialty suppliers in the United States, once noted, "The Corvette is a *lifestyle*."

BIRTH OF AN AMERICAN DREAM

Chevrolet, long the champion of affordable transportation for the masses, was fast rising to the top of the heap in postwar car design by the early 1950s. In 1951, GM's soon-to-be legendary design chief, Harley Earl, saw the potential for a personal-sized roadster in the American market. Witnessing the popularity of the many British roadsters coming ashore in America, Earl saw a demand for a style of car that Chevrolet lacked in its product line. Earl believed, too, that for the most part the British cars were underpowered and overpriced. He sensed that a sports car offering a combination of American value and power along with the European qualities that made these cars appealing would be a sure bet on the U.S. market. Earl envisioned an accessible roadster priced in the $1,800 to $1,900 range—similar in cost to an MG at the time.

The first Corvette roadster, offered in 1953, lived up to Earl's expectations in some aspects, and fell painfully short in others. At $3,498 base, the price tag was far above what Earl had envisioned—the cost of developing a new, smaller frame for the roadster-sized Corvette added dollars to the price tag. Yet the Corvette's handsome design was distinctive. Four small fins surrounded the taillights, examples of Earl's interest in aviation design and a restrained version of what was to follow from Detroit. European-inspired elements such as Le Mans–styled wire-mesh stone guards over the headlights further enhanced its race-car styling, but the Corvette still lacked the daring of other roadsters of the era, notably the Jaguar XK-120. Its fiberglass construction was a first for one of the major automakers, but it took Chevrolet a bit longer than anticipated to perfect the process of working with the new material.

Perhaps Chevrolet's biggest error was in its choice of transmission. While the in-line six engine produced the desired 150 horsepower, it was transferred to the rear wheels via a lethargic two-speed automatic transmission. Performance was, as a result, conservative at best, and the automatic transmission and subsequent lack of power held little appeal for the ripe roadster market. Fewer than 350 Corvettes were delivered in 1953, as manufacturing difficulties encountered in working with the fiberglass slowed, and at times halted, production. Handling was not up to expectations, and power was lacking, but Chevrolet did begin to mold and shape the aura that would forever surround the Corvette. Minor changes for the 1954 model brought about an increase in sales for that first full year of production, but with 3,640 units built and 1,100 of those left unsold at year's end Chevrolet was far from satisfied.

It was GM's brilliant engineer Zora Arkus-Duntov who convinced the company to keep the marque alive. Duntov put power under the Corvette's hood: he tuned the chassis to give the '55 Corvette real sports-car handling, and added an optional 265-cubic-inch engine that pumped out a respectable 195 horsepower and a three-speed manual gearbox. But in spite of improved performance and handling, Corvette sales were still far below what was expected by the brain trust on the top floor of the GM corporate headquarters—only seven hundred cars were produced, making the 1955 the second rarest of all Corvettes.

THE CORVETTE COMES OF AGE

It is a widely held belief that, were it not for Ford's successful introduction of their own Thunderbird roadster the same year, Chevrolet might have given up on the roadster market after 1955. Instead, the company moved forward with a completely redesigned Corvette for 1956, and that second-generation body is still regarded as one of Corvette's finest designs. With a shape and proportions that were close to perfect, and attractive side coves that allowed for stunning two-tone paint jobs, the '56 was a perfect blend of European and U.S. design cues. In terms of the car's performance, both handling and horsepower increased under Duntov's careful engineering.

The '57 Corvette remained relatively unchanged from the '56 on the outside, but performance was greatly improved. For the first time on a Corvette, a manual four-speed gearbox was offered (although the two-speed automatic still lingered on),

as well as a choice of several power options under the hood. The Corvette—still under the keen eye of Duntov—was developing into a genuine sports car as defined by the European makers. In roadster form, there were few cars, if any, produced in the United States at the time that were as beautiful.

From 1958 through 1960, following the trend in American car design, more chrome and questionable design themes detracted from the classic, no-nonsense lines of the beauties of 1956 and '57. Four headlights, louvers on the hood (which thankfully lasted only for the 1958 model), and an overabundance of chrome watered down an otherwise fine design. In 1960, Corvette broke the 300 horsepower mark with an optional engine package, setting the standard for future Corvette models: a powerful, stump-pulling V-8 engine.

The year 1961 saw the introduction of a restyled Corvette, though mechanical changes were few on the new model. Under the tutelage of new GM styling chief

William "Bill" Mitchell, and with limited funds available for a completely new design, the '61 emerged as a masterful blend of the best lines of the '56 along with a sleek new rear end derived from the SS racing car. The '61 and '62 Corvettes, particularly the roadster—with the top down, of course—were and remain jewels to behold. In 1962 few changes were made to the body style, but an optional 360hp engine yielded scorching zero-to-sixty times in the mid–five second range. *Power* and Corvette were becoming synonymous. But it was the '62 Corvette roadster that endeared itself to the U.S. public at large, via the television exploits of Martin Milner and Kent McCord in the successful series *Route 66*.

THE STING RAY STRIKES

In 1963 Chevrolet released a totally new Corvette, completely revised aesthetically and mechanically from the frame up. Called the Sting Ray, this stunning body style—

available as either a coupe or a roadster—would run through 1967. Perhaps best known for the one-year-only split rear window (featured on the 1963 models) that was the most memorable feature of the coupe, the roadster continued to outsell the coupe through 1968. The '63 Sting Ray also featured an independent rear suspension, in 1965, the big-block engine became an option, providing satisfied drivers with a whopping 425 horsepower and solidifying the Corvette's standing as a serious American sports car.

By the late 1960s, government safety and emissions regulations caused U.S. manufacturers as much consternation as they did their overseas counterparts. Although Chevrolet's designers were able to integrate new bumpers more gracefully than had the European automakers, engine regulations took a heavy toll, as horsepower figures began to drop, especially on the standard engine. In 1968, it was a healthy 300 horsepower; by 1975, following the gas crisis and stopgap emission controls, which both suffocated and starved engines, horsepower plummeted to a numbing 150hp in a car that had also grown consistently heavier each year.

Advances in emission-control technology in the late 1970s allowed Corvette to recoup some of its lost power. In 1975 Chevrolet decided to drop the roadster from the following year's Corvette line. Sales had dropped to around 2,600 units and it was assumed at the time that the government was about to mandate strict rollover standards for convertibles, a standard that Corvette could not have met without a major redesign. Chevrolet dropped the roadster and replaced it with a T-Top. While it still provided open-air fun, the T-Top was a far cry from the traditional, almost romantic query, "Shall we put the top down?" When Corvette dropped the convertible many believed the end of the roadster was close at hand.

DECLINE AND REBIRTH

Corvette soldiered on through the late 1970s with redesigns and retunings, and the power fluctuations that invariably accompany such changes.

While performance remained brisk and the T-Top appealed to many customers, no roadsters were available. A completely new Corvette was introduced in 1984: it was now smaller overall, but with more interior space. Initially no roadster was available, but Chevy caught on and reintroduced the Corvette roadster in 1986. In 1988 a turbocharged Corvette roadster restored some of the missing horsepower that had been the hallmark of earlier Corvettes and Sting Rays. The turbocharger was fast becoming recognized as a clean and cheap way to get more power out of engines—emissions didn't suffer, nor was fuel mileage impacted greatly with an increase in power of some 100 horsepower. Chevrolet contracted independent supplier Reeves Callaway to do the engine modifications by adding the turbochargers, and the Calloway engine mods were available as an option on new Vettes. Longtime fans of high-horsepower Vettes finally had something under the hood to smile about again.

Corvette had survived throughout model changes, ups and downs in the economy, changing regulations, and years of corporate chaos at the top of GM America's only true sports car. At the end of the 1980s, it was feared that General Motors—suffering from a variety of maladies as a result of mismanagement, poor product lines, and shoddy quality control as well as an apparent inability to assess market trends—would eliminate the Corvette altogether. Surprisingly, what emerged was an entirely new, groundbreaking Corvette. As we'll discuss later, this time the gifted and talented Corvette project team would make a roadster that would live up to the Vette's longtime reputation as America's favorite sports car, creating a truly world-class sports car, the C-5.

LEFT: *Because of the three-to four-year styling cycle then in place at GM, the original Sting Ray would bow out in 1967. In spite of its brief, four-year run, the Sting Ray, whether coupe or roadster, remains one of the Corvettes most sought after by Vette aficionados. From this side view of a fine '67 roadster, it is easy to see why.*

OPPOSITE: *In 1973 and '74 the Sting Ray's thin chrome bumpers were gone, replaced by the color-matched rubber bumpers required by government regulations. Under the hood, tamed emissions were robbing Corvette of what it was famous for, stump-pulling V-8 power. Unlike other roadsters from the period, which faded and died, the Corvette thrived, celebrating a rebirth in the 1980s.*

ABOVE: *Decked out in all of the chrome accouterments that defined 1950s auto styling, this 1956 is a fine example of a well-optioned Bird. Wire wheels, wide whitewalls, a Continental spare tire mount, and lots of shiny trim loaded questionable '50s taste onto a handsome design.*

OPPOSITE: *All three roadster models of the two-seater T-Birds—1955, 1956, and 1957—line up in a classic pose. All that's missing are the car hops.*

FORD ANSWERS BACK

General Motors was not the only one of the Big Three automakers to take notice of those little British roadsters that were so in much demand in the States in the early 1950s. Ford decided that they, too, would tap into the fast-growing roadster market with a unique little two-seater of their own.

THE THUNDERBIRD LANDS

The last major American entry into the roadster market, the Thunderbird, made a bigger splash than any car that had preceded it, when it was introduced in 1955. Offering more power than the struggling Corvette, and featuring enough creature comforts to appeal to the mass market—including windows that actually rolled up and down and a luxurious interior—the first Thunderbird was an immediate hit. And unlike the Corvette, it was built primarily from parts and engines readily available from a variety of Ford cars.

Raw power was never a strong suit of the early Thunderbirds, although a supercharged engine in the '57 put out a respectable 325 horsepower. Unfortunately the chassis and suspension were never quite up to getting that power to the ground, especially on winding roads—the domain of true sports cars. A real roadster, the Thunderbird was a decent straight-line performer, but its handling didn't inspire confidence, even in the most skilled drivers. Offering a softer ride than the racing-derived suspension of the Vette, the Thunderbird was more at home cruising on the new systems of interstate highways that were beginning to thread their way across the North American landscape than it was taking on a challenging backcountry road. Nevertheless, the Thunderbird outsold the Corvette each year, primarily due to the T-Bird's advantages in sleek styling and power—which must have caused fits of hair-pulling and teeth-gnashing at GM.

T-Bird styling during those early years followed the rest of the auto industry, mimicking aircraft, which in the mid-1950s were swept back, razor sharp, and jet powered. The 1956 roadster's pretty, removable hardtop featured optional circular opera windows that became a distinctive spotting feature, and a rear-mounted Continental kit. A 1957 redesign gave the Thunderbird more pronounced, knife-edged tail fins; that model is widely regarded as the most beautiful T-Bird ever built, and a classic of U.S. auto design.

The Thunderbird may be regarded as the first truly successful American roadster. In its first year, more than sixteen thousand Thunderbirds found their way into U.S. garages (while Chevy struggled to move just seven hundred Corvettes), and in 1957 the number increased to more than twenty-one thousand T-Birds sold. Impressive as these numbers were, Ford's upper management felt that the car would sell better if it could increase the Thunderbird's customer base to include families, something the classic two-seat roadster did not really support. Thus, 1957 was the last year for the short-lived Thunderbird roadster. In 1958 the T-bird grew into an overweight four-seat convertible. It was extremely successful, but it was the end of the roadster line for Ford; not until the next century would the Blue Oval appear on another two-seat roadster: a new Thunderbird for the new millennium.

PAGES 68–69: *In 1955, Ford released the stylish Thunderbird, its answer to the Corvette. To everyone's surprise, since it lacked the Vette's performance, the Thunderbird went on to outsell its rival. Perhaps the answer lay in its trim and stylish design, which the Vette would challenge with its own handsome image in the next few years.*

OPPOSITE: *Coming or going, the 1957 T-Bird exhibited well-balanced and very attractive design; its conservative deployment of chrome is especially commendable, considering what it shared road space with that year. Garish design and an overabundance of chrome were de rigueur, but, happily the Bird was spared those indignities.*

LEFT, TOP AND BOTTOM: *The signature Thunderbird porthole hardtop was a popular option in regions where the seasons changed. Why stop driving your T-Bird when winter howled in?*

BELOW: *What the exterior of the 1957 lacked in chrome, the designers made up for in the interior. The instrument cluster was attractive, however, and seemed to borrow heavily from European designs. The deep-dish steering wheel was signature Ford.*

WHEN AC MET FORD: MR. SHELBY'S COBRA

The Shelby Cobra, one of the most celebrated and sought-after American roadsters of the 1960s, was not really an American automobile at all. This unique hybrid of British styling and American muscle was the brainchild of a successful U.S. racecar driver. Today, Carroll Shelby and the Cobra name are twin stars in the annals of American sports cars. A true rags-to-riches story, Shelby started out as a chicken farmer, got into sports car racing, and eventually came to design one of the finest U.S. roadsters ever built. Flamboyant and innovative, he became a legend in his own time.

Ever mindful of the credo that "nothing is better than more horsepower," English manufacturer AC Motors had lost their engine supplier for their AC Ace roadster in 1961. Visionary Shelby saw the potential for marrying the English AC Ace with the then new Ford 260-cubic-inch lightweight V-8, and approached AC and Ford with the idea. Luckily, both companies were agreeable to his concept—AC needed an engine and Ford needed a high-profile sports car to show off their new high-horsepower engine, which was being manufactured for their own Falcon sedan. The name Cobra came to Shelby in a dream, and the legend of Cobra was born. *Sports Car Graphic* magazine, in an initial road test of the Cobra, described the acceleration of this new car as "*explosive!*"

Over its production run from 1962 to '68, the engine bay housed the Ford 289 engine and, finally, the one most desired by Cobra enthusiasts, the mighty 427. The 427 put out almost 400 horsepower, but in a crude chassis: only the most skilled drivers could exact the best performance out of the overpowered, and under-chassised monster.

Racing, though, is where the Cobra earned its reputation. In its first outing, the Cobra—with almost a one-ton weight advantage over the heavier Corvette—handily trounced its GM rival. Cobras were entered in most European long-distance racing events and the car's illustrious career reached its apogee in 1964. At the '64 24 Hours of Le Mans a Cobra finished fourth overall and beat the factory Ferraris for first overall in the GT class. In 1965 Cobra won the FIA Touring Car Championship, the only American car ever to do so.

The commitment to lots of horsepower, along with the Shelby name, made the Cobra so successful that replicas of the car are still manufactured today by a variety of makers. The concept of a monster engine in a small, nimble roadster would not take shape until the 1990s, when Chrysler unleashed the Cobra-inspired Viper.

OPPOSITE: *Few cars from the 1960s stirred the soul more and induced more fits of released testosterone than the 427 Shelby Cobra. Frighteningly fast and unforgiving when out of sorts at speed, it was raw American horsepower mated with an English chassis and body. This across-the-Pond hybrid was the brainchild of Carroll Shelby.*

RIGHT: *The English AC logo with the American Cobra logo of Carroll Shelby above marked an automotive marriage second to none.*

BELOW: *How many adjectives and adverbs can you bestow upon this car in sixty seconds? There simply was no more aggressive-looking car around in 1966, when this Mark III with a Holman Moody 302 engine was released. Even its staunch Italian rival, Ferrari—the marque Shelby set out to beat with the Cobra—had no car this fierce-looking in its competition lineup.*

ABOVE: *The 1953 Nash-Healey was a hybrid sports car that featured a body by Pininfarina, a chassis and assembly by English manufacturer Donald Healey, and an American Nash six-cylinder engine. The U.S. manufacturer hoped that the Nash Healey would endow their otherwise mundane product line of sedans with an image of performance, and breathe some life into it. The high-priced automobile never caught on with the otherwise car-starved buying public of the early 1950s.*

OPPOSITE: *The design of the Nash-Healey was pure Pininfarina, and, had the automaker dropped the Nash-styled grille, the car would have looked as good from the front as from the rear. Beating the Corvette into production by a few months, the Nash-Healey claimed to be the first true sports car from the United States.*

LITTLE CARS FROM LITTLE COMPANIES

There were some rather strange, memorable, and, yes, even forgettable roadster offerings produced in the United States during the decade following World War II. Some of these rare and obscure cars that were borne on the wings of the seemingly limitless optimism of postwar America may not have been as successful as the Thunderbird or the Corvette, but they made a splash nonetheless, and had an influence on the market in general. Although they came and went, often in small numbers, those early independents were genuine attempts to produce an entirely American brand of roadster.

CROSLEY

Here is a great cocktail-party trivia question: "What was the first true American roadster built after World War II?" Chances are, ninety-nine percent of the answers will be either the Chevrolet Corvette or the Ford Thunderbird. But truth doesn't always lie in numbers, and the truth is that the first American roadster did not come from one of Detroit's so-called Big Three.

The first roadster produced in the United States was the Crosley Hot Shot/Super Sport, manufactured from 1946 to 1952. Millionaire Powell Crosley manufactured small, motorcycle engine–powered cars just prior to the war; after the war, he acquired rights to one of the many military surplus engines that were available, a diminutive 722 cc overhead-cam four-cylinder. Using this engine and a common platform, Crosley produced an entire line of various-bodied cars and light trucks, and a pair of roadsters—the Hot Shot and the nearly identical Super Sport. The Hot Shot/Super Sport seemed to borrow and mimic lines from a myriad of British cars. Differences between the two models were slight: the Super Sport had doors, the Hot Shot cut-down side panels.

A spotting feature of any Crosley is a tiny chromed spinning propeller mounted on the grille. Aviation was first and foremost on the minds of Americans after the vital role it had played in bringing victory to the Allies; that tiny propeller on all model Crosley grilles was a foreshadowing of the aviation influence that would manifest itself as garish fins, intakes, and grilles on all American auto designs in the 1950s.

Power for the Crosley was a meager 26 horsepower, although aftermarket parts suppliers and speed shops got that figure up to over 50hp. The car was bare-bones simple in terms of construction, cheap to operate, and very reliable. There were some engineering advancements in the Crosley, though, including disc brakes—Crosley, in 1949, was the first U.S. automaker to offer these on a production car. However, after a mere two years, the disc brakes were dropped, as they were unreliable and had a propensity to lock up and seize at the most inopportune times. Production reverted to tried and proven drum brakes for the remainder of Crosley's existence.

All Crosley production ceased in 1952. The heady and wildly optimistic postwar American philosophy of "bigger is best" relegated the Crosley to being seen as somewhat toylike when compared to the enormous, heavy, and highly desirable land yachts that had begun rolling off U.S. assembly lines.

KAISER–DARRIN

Industrialist Henry Kaiser made his fortune in cement and the creative manufacturing of Victory Ships assembly line–style for the war effort. For a decade after the war, Kaiser produced automobiles, for the most part sedans and coupes in a variety of startlingly unconventional designs for the period. Kaiser had his own way of doing things, and if performance was not a strong suit of the Kaisers, their sleek and flowing shape certainly was. Kaisers looked like nothing else rolling down any road.

ABOVE: *The Crosley was way ahead of its time, a small car in a land yacht age. Bashful beside the slightly stodgy convertible is the endearing Hot Shot.*

OPPOSITE: *Produced in 1953 and '54, the daring Kaiser-Darrin roadster was the work of California designer Howard "Dutch" Darrin. Its engineering didn't live up to its design: under-powered, with an anemic Willys 90-hp, six-cylinder engine under the hood, fewer than five hundred rolled off the assembly line before the car was axed from the Kaiser lineup.*

Designer Dutch Darrin had proposed a design study for Kaiser called the Blue Car. It was to be a convertible built on a shortened Kaiser sedan frame and powered by a V-8 engine. In retrospect, the Blue Car had the potential on paper to be the Mustang of its time, but Kaiser rejected the design and instead produced the small Henry J sedan at exactly the same time as bigger cars began to herald the preferred style of the day.

Working independently from the "shipbuilding" mind-set infecting Kaiser automobiles, Dutch Darrin designed a roadster based on the Henry J chassis. That roadster, the Kaiser-Darrin, was sleek and captivating, unlike anything ever seen before. Constructed of fiberglass, it featured doors that slid open, and was the star of the auto show circuit in 1952. Powered by a 90 horsepower engine, its performance was adequate at best, but handling was fine as the Henry J chassis was beefed up for better road holding.

The downside to the Kaiser-Darrin, which probably led to its demise, was its high cost. The little roadster fell in the price range of the performance-oriented Lincoln Capri and of some Cadillacs, at a time when value for dollars was measured by the size of the car and the reputation of the marque. Unfortunately for Kaiser, a two-seat fiberglass roadster made by a small and little-known manufacturer did not stack up to a Cadillac, which was big, impressive, and available at the same price. Production ceased after a mere 435 units. But, the stunning Kaiser-Darrin did offer the roadster experience in a United States that was slowly coming around to appreciating that special driving pleasure.

THE NASH-HEALEY

Though, like the Kaiser-Darrin, it was small in actual production numbers, mention must be made of the Nash-Healey roadster. Born of an idea that sprang from a shipboard meeting between Donald Healey and George Mason of Nash Kelvinator

onboard HMS *Queen Elizabeth* between Southampton and New York, it was an attempt to market a roadster in the United States before Detroit's Big Three could. The Nash-Healey, which appeared in 1950, was the first of several across-the-Pond hybrids that combined an American engine with a European body and chassis. An American-made Nash 3.6-liter six-cylinder engine powered a body and chassis designed and manufactured by Donald Healey.

The Nash-Healey roadster's initial design was not well received, and sales amounted to only a little over a hundred units. While figures like this were fine for a cottage industry like Healey, Nash Kelvinator was accustomed to bigger sales and far greater profits. In 1951 production was halted and noted Italian designer Pininfarina did a complete redesign. Though attractive, the new car provided only moderate performance, and (once the cost of shipping the car to the States was factored in) the price was higher than anything else in its class, which further hurt sales.

Nash-Healeys finished fourth in 1950 and third in 1953 in the 24 Hours of Le Mans. Production ceased in 1954 with roughly five hundred cars being sold. By then serious competition was on the horizon: the XK-120 had landed on U.S. shores and the standard of what a roadster should be had shifted to Jaguar.

chapter FIVE

ITALIAN SPEED

f automobiles are a passion in the United States, in Italy they are nothing short of an obsession. Italy is home to such distinguished marques as Ferrari, Maserati, Alfa Romeo, and Lamborghini, and to such cutting-edge and trend-setting design studios as Pininfarina, Vignale, Michelotti, and Bertone. It is home, too, to such legendary racing venues as the Mille Miglia, Targa Florio, and Monza, and its champion race drivers—Ascari, Nuvolari, Farina, Taruffi, Bandini, and, of course, Andretti—are regarded as near mythical, the saints of the track.

Based on U.S. television ratings and marketing campaigns, one might assume that NASCAR is the world's most popular racing series. But in Italy, the overall emotional well-being of an entire nation hinges on the fortunes of Ferrari as

PREVIOUS PAGE: *Named for Enzo Ferrari's son, Dino, who died in 1956, this 1970 Ferrari 246GT Dino was a departure for Ferrari. The car was powered by a V6 instead of the mandatory V12, and it lacked the Ferrari Prancing Horse emblem. Never as popular as its pricier twelve-cylinder siblings, it did, however, offer the Ferrari mystique more affordably.*

ABOVE: *The Spartan 1948 Ferrari 166 Spyder Corsa, built strictly for competition, was never meant to be a road car. The cockpit was a perfect "office," its function simple and efficient, with nothing to distract the driver.*

ABOVE RIGHT: *Clean, yet aggressive design is the hallmark of Ferrari's 166 series, intended for racing. Powered by a 2-liter single overhead cam V12, the 166 won just about every race it entered, including Le Mans and the Mille Miglia. The fenders and headlamps were removable, so the car could compete in Formula events as well as those for sports cars.*

OPPOSITE: *The Ferrari 860 Monza first appeared in 1955 at the Tourist Trophy race. Notable on the 860 was the four-cylinder engine, which, for the first time in Ferrari sports racers, featured a stroke greater than the bore.*

it contests the Formula One championship every other Sunday during the season. In Maranello, home to Ferrari, a win on any track means a day-into-evening celebration throughout the streets of the town. Should a Ferrari win the Italian Grand Prix at Monza, the spectacle of the vast legions of *tifosi* swarming onto the track as the checkered flag falls is a mere prelude to the festivities carried on nationwide. Is it any wonder with this rich racing background that the roadsters produced in Italy—known there as *spyders*—inspire the same degree of passion?

FERRARI

No automobile maker inspires quite the same passion and admiration as the venerable Ferrari company. Perhaps it is the automaker's strong racing lineage that inspires its legions of fans. Indeed, racing was the primary reason for Ferrari's existence: founder Enzo Ferrari—who never finished engineering school—began his career with dreams of racing, and was soon testing cars on the track for such Italian automakers as Alfa Romeo in the 1920s. After years in the ranks at Alfa Romeo, he lit out on his own in 1938 and formed Società Auto-Avio Costruzione Ferrari. The house became one of the most respected makers of race cars, and success on the

track translated into profits, used to produce a limited amount of special road cars. During the 1950s, production of such cars became a sideline to racing for Ferrari.

Ferraris are among those rare and magic automobiles that have an ability to capture the soul of a driver, even after only the briefest of encounters. Seeing a Ferrari on the road—as opposed to on the track—is not an everyday or even weekly event. (Of course should you live in Maranello or near Rodeo Drive in Los Angeles, you stand a much better chance of sighting the famous yellow and black Prancing Horse badge.) This author can vividly recall just about every Ferrari I've seen on the road in the past twenty or so years, and can tell you where, when, and what model. That's how rare and memorable a roadgoing Ferrari is. When one pulls up beside me, as has happened on a few spellbinding occasions, I turn off any music playing on the stereo, silence my traveling companion, and roll down the window, enthralled by the harmony of the twelve-cylinder exhaust note. (V-8-powered Ferraris, although wonderful to see, do not inspire the same level of enchantment as the exhaust symphony of twelve-cylinder variants.)

Ferraris have been low-volume handmade cars for all but the most recent decade. Not an everyman's everyday car, Ferraris have been sold to entertainers,

sports figures, artists, and those knowledgeable millionaires who can afford to drive such an exotic car. And many such lucky individuals choose to enhance the sheer ecstasy of driving one of the world's finest automobiles with the thrill of the open air. While Ferrari roadsters are surprisingly rare, no book on roadsters would be complete without coverage of this celebrated marque.

Most of the roadgoing Ferraris produced have been coupes, two-plus-twos, and four-passenger convertibles; the few roadsters built by the company were produced in very low numbers. Ferrari's first roadster was the 166/166 MM, manufactured between 1947 and 1953. It featured what was to become Ferrari's signature engine under the hood, a V-12, and was primarily a race car, winning at Le Mans and the Mille Miglia. The 212 Export followed, and common chassis and V-12 engines were custom-bodied by a variety of Italian designers.

The 342 America, produced between 1950 and '55, was Ferrari's first crack at the U.S. market. Enzo Ferrari felt that the United States was ready for something more than the buzzy though peppy four-cylinder cars arriving from Europe. Horsepower was to be the 342 America's selling point, and to achieve this the then-current V-12 Formula One engine—rated at 230 horsepower—went under the hood. Pininfarina

built all bodies for the 342, which included a small number of roadsters, a sleek fast-back coupe, and a less sleek two-plus-two coupe. Subsequent Ferrari roadsters for the balance of the '50s and early '60s were built strictly for racing.

In 1968 the design studio Scaglietti built ten roadsters/convertibles on the 275GTB chassis for Luigi Chinetti, the longtime Greenwich, Connecticut–based importer of Ferraris, and the American home of Ferrari racing. Power for this stunning roadster came from a 260 horsepower V-12 that was downgraded slightly from the coupe's engine. In the ensuing years Ferrari production was based on coupes and on two-plus-two convertibles with a smattering of one-off or extremely low-volume roadsters for clients who wanted only a roadster and could ante up the lire.

The Testa Rossa of 1984 was to be Ferrari's next true roadster produced in any kind of numbers. Designed again by one of Ferrari's favorite designers, Pininfarina, the car was large by Ferrari standards. Weight savings were realized by aluminum body construction, and the 380 horsepower four-cam engine was good for a top speed of over 180 miles per hour (290kph). When compared to other Ferrari roadsters, the Testa Rossa might be considered almost common, as production numbers were quite high compared to the company's other roadster models, but there is nothing like it in the realm of roadsters.

When Enzo Ferrari died in 1988 at the age of ninety, the Ferrari faithful worried that the company would fold without the guiding hand and tutelage of its founder. The firm fell under the corporate umbrella of Fiat, which brought new and modern production technology to Ferrari, and helped fund its Formula One team.

ABOVE LEFT: *The ex–Rob Walker 196S Dino roadster, powered by the 246 six-cylinder engine, was raced in the capable hands of the late Rodriguez brothers, Ricardo and Pedro. Who wouldn't want to slide behind the wheel of this thoroughbred, fire up the engine, and attempt a flat-out lap around Monza or the Nurburgring?*

LEFT: *The 1959 Ferrari California Spyder was a variation on the 250 GT series produced between 1954 and 1962; as the name implies, the car was designed with the U.S. market in mind. Built on the 250GT competition chassis that saw wins in the Tour de France, it flaunted a performance that matched its choice design. Was there a finer car in which to cruise up and down California's Coast Highway in 1959?*

OPPOSITE: *Ferrari released the F-50 in 1996 to celebrate the firm's fiftieth anniversary. Styled by Pininfarina, the F-50 was the closest a driver with extremely deep pockets could get to driving a Formula One car on the road. Powered by a detuned V-12 from the then-current Formula One, the F-50 touched a top speed of more than 200 miles per hour (321.8kph).*

FIAT

Today a large multinational corporation, Fiat started as an automobile manufacturer way back in 1899. While never a big player in the U.S. market, Fiat exported a range of roadsters to the United States from 1959 up until the early 1980s. Never strong on reliability—a running joke among car enthusiasts says that the firm's name stands for "Fix it again today?"—Fiat roadsters nonetheless garnered a small but faithful following. Nimble handling, high-revving overhead-cam four-cylinder engines plus a driving position that can best be described as "classic Italian arms-out" made for a series of roadsters that often outperformed their British counterparts.

One of the first Fiat roadsters available in the United States was the 1100, produced in 1959, albeit in very small numbers. It was a very stylish and unique-looking car in its time, although its Pininfarina-designed body might be regarded as more stately than sporting. Power was adequate, as was the car's handling. Top end was around 85 miles per hour (135kph), and zero-to-sixty times were lengthy to say the least. The 1100 evolved into the more sporty and again Pininfarina-designed

1200 in 1959 and 1500 in '63. These cars reflected the fine design lines and shapes that were the hallmark of Pininfarina. It wasn't until the late 1960s, with the introduction of the 850 Spyder and the 124 series roadster, that Fiat gained any significant sales numbers in the United States.

The 850 Spyder, designed by Bertone, was built on the Fiat 850 sedan chassis. The engine, which produced a meager 54 horsepower, was mounted in the rear and propelled the 850 from zero to sixty in a patient eighteen-plus seconds. No matter, the 850 was a good seller for Fiat. What it lacked in overall performance was made up for with fine styling and a modest price.

The Fiat 124 Spyder and its counterpart, the two-plus-two coupe, are the Fiat sports cars most remembered. The 124 roadster, or "Spyder" in Fiat jargon, landed on U.S. shores in 1968. It was attractive and offered as standard items not available in competitors' roadsters: a five-speed gearbox and disc brakes on all four wheels. The twin overhead-cam four-cylinder engine was free-revving and produced 96 horsepower and a respectable zero-to-sixty time of twelve and a half seconds.

Somehow, though, the spirited sound of the four-cylinder always gave drivers the impression that they were motoring much faster than what the speedometer read. Handling was superb in any 124 Spyder, even if the steeply angled steering wheel seemed more suited to a bus than to a sports car—it was because of this strangely angled steering wheel on the Fiat (as well as contemporary Alfa Romeos) that the "arms out" driving-style term was coined.

Changes to the 124 Spyder over the course of its production run up to 1985 were mostly cosmetic. The engines rose in power each year, peaking at 108hp in 1973, but governmental regulations in the United States changed the bumpers, and emissions requirements led to the first real decrease in power, which dropped to 96hp in 1974. Happily, in 1982 fuel injection and turbocharging brought the power back up to 120hp.

In 1984 Fiat ended its production of sports cars and exited the U.S. market, though the 124 Spyder remained in the United States for one more year directly under the Pininfarina label.

OPPOSITE TOP: *The lovely 1958 Fiat 1200-TV convertible, designed by Pininfarina, sold for about the same price as a Chevrolet Impala convertible or a Triumph TR-3. Its selling points were its sporty looks, smooth free-revving engine, and supple ride. However, it possessed neither the size nor the power of the Impala, nor did it come close to the TR-3's performance level, making it a tough sell to an American market giddy over performance.*

OPPOSITE BOTTOM: *With a special body by Italian designer Vignale, this 1954 Fiat Spyder looked more like a Ferrari than the everyday, bread-and-butter cars that Fiat usually produced.*

LEFT: *Beginning in 1963, Fiat produced the Dino Spyder, which featured a Ferrari 206 Dino V-6 engine. The Fiat Dino was an expensive hybrid, with a price tag way above what one ever expected to pay for a Fiat, even one with a Ferrari engine under the hood. In 1969, Fiat and Ferrari merged, and by 1970, the year of this model, Ferrari was building the cars at Maranello alongside their own Dino.*

Alfa Romeo

Perhaps the most romantic-sounding name in the entire auto industry, Alfa Romeo dates to the dawn of the twentieth century, when engineer Nicola Romeo took over Anonima Lombarda Fabbrica Automobili (ALFA). The firm established a formidable reputation during the 1920s and '30s with some of the best cars on the racetrack, consistently outperforming entries from Mercedes-Benz, Bugatti, and Bentley.

As successful as Alfa was on the track, the firm didn't get into mass production until a decade after World War II. Starting in 1954 Alfa began to produce a line of coupes and roadsters that would become, in spite of finicky reliability, some of the most highly regarded sports cars to come out of Italy.

The Giulietta Spyder and Spyder Veloce of 1955 were Alfa Romeo's first true roadsters, convertible versions of the Giulietta Sprint and Sprint Veloce. Like all Alfas to follow, the spyder variants had elegant design and great performance for cars of their size and engine displacement. In '58 the 2000 Spyder was introduced, an offshoot of the larger Super Sprint coupe. This model saw a floor shift for the first time in an Alfa. Though more powerful than the Giulietta roadsters, the weight of the 2000 made it slower and less nimble than its smaller sibling. The Giulia Spyder, introduced in 1962, was favored for its small size and taut suspension, which, combined with its 112 horsepower, yielded a fantastic driver's car.

The next Alfa roadster was the Duetto, introduced in 1966. Immortalized in the 1967 film *The Graduate*, the Duetto was a legend in its own time, and is still considered by many to be the finest-designed Alfa spyder ever. Under its profoundly sexy skin was a 109 horsepower dual overhead-cam four, which gave a zero-to-sixty time of eleven-plus seconds and a top end of more than 115 miles per hour (185kph). In 1967 the rear end suffered the indignity of having its curvaceous contours chopped off and replaced with a flat Kamm back tail that forever killed the

almost perfect design of the Duetto. It was claimed that improved aerodynamics were the reason behind this radical bit of surgery.

(It should be noted that Porsche, under the engineering vision of John Wyer, did the same thing to their new and troublesome 917 race car in 1970. The 917 had an alarming propensity to become unstable at high speeds—and even became airborne on the three-mile-long Mulsanne Straight at Le Mans. John Wyer Engineering of England had taken over the 917 factory effort, and in testing the 917 Wyer's team discovered that better stability and a higher top speed could be achieved by chopping off the long tail. When the rear was chopped off into a Kamm back, the results were

OPPOSITE: *While legendary Italian driver Tazio Nuvolari was making a winning name for Alfa with its P-2 at the Targa Florio and Mille Miglia, the public was being offered the 8C-2300 roadster.*

RIGHT TOP: *The swept-back grille of this vintage two-seater built for speed and performance is signature Alfa Romeo.*

RIGHT BOTTOM: *Prone to rust, the 1961 Alfa Giulietta Spyder is an increasingly rare car to see nowadays. Possessing the sex appeal inherent to Alfa roadsters, the popular Giulietta accounted for much of Alfa's growth between 1955 and 1960.*

ABOVE: *"Where have you gone, Mrs. Robinson?" The Alfa Romeo that caught the attention of U.S. car buyers was the Spyder Veloce, the automotive star of the hit movie The Graduate. With a stunning body by Pininfarina, it was one of the most beautiful Alfas ever produced.*

OPPOSITE: *This 1994 Alfa Romeo convertible traces its roots to the Spyder Veloce opposite. In an attempt to keep the car contemporary, designers chopped the sweeping, streamlined body at the rear, tacked on trim hither and yon, and gave the car color-keyed rubber bumpers.*

startling—they won the 24 Hours of Le Mans plus just about every race the 917 entered for the next few years. As a result the 917 is today regarded as one of the all-time greatest Porsche race cars ever. Thus, Alfa Romeo may actually and surprisingly have had reasons beyond aesthetics for their "chop" job.)

In the early 1980s, the Alfa got a rubber-nose treatment in order to meet the stringent regulations then being imposed by the U.S. government, though the change was infinitely more tasteful than the unfortunate MGB's nose job a few years prior.

Alfa Romeo, while never a high-volume car in the United States, offered the roadster experience in a range of exciting models with a decidedly Italian flair and personality. Remaining Alfas are few and far between today, unfortunately, as their bodies had a nasty habit of rusting at a most rapid pace.

chapter SIX

GERMAN ENGINEERING

Germany has produced and continues to make some of the finest road cars in the world. From small family sedans to sports cars with capabilities far beyond the capacities of average drivers, inherent performance and handling characteristics have become a standard for German automakers. Germany itself offers driving conditions unlike those found anywhere else—there are no speed limits on Germany's autobahns, which wind along the mountainous Alpine switchbacks that shaped the German auto industry and made their cars such a pleasure to drive. Teutonic engineering,

PREVIOUS PAGES: *From the first, the name Carrera signified Porsche's special, high-performance variation of its stock model. This 1957 Speedster featured a larger, tuned 1.6-liter flat-four engine.*

ABOVE: *The year 1955 was the last year the 356 model was produced prior to the improved 356A. The car's pristine lines, sans rear bumpers, and its utilitarian cockpit design are in keeping with the responsive handling that is characteristic of all Porsche models.*

OPPOSITE: *The legendary 718RSK Porsche was built for the track; behind the wheel sat some of the most notable drivers of the time, stars such as Sterling Moss, Wolfgang Von Trips, Ken Miles, and Dan Gurney. Though small in size and engine displacement, the RSK handily beat cars twice as powerful—thus establishing Porsche's reputation on the track.*

recognized for its precision and craftsmanship, garners immediate respect and awe among enthusiasts.

Although there are relatively few German roadsters, they rank among the finest ever made. Mercedes continues its roadster tradition, which began with the 190SL in 1954; the company would always have a roadster in its product line, on through to the present day. BMW offered the 507 for a brief period but concentrated its efforts on the sedan line. And Porsche emerged from the ashes of World War II to become a sports car icon. As we drive into the new millennium, it is Germany that is defining the standard of performance and design for all the world to follow. But to appreciate its leadership today a ride in some memorable and highly prized German roadsters is in order.

PORSCHE

It's been said that there are sports cars and then there are Porsches. Some might disagree, but even the harshest critic will be smiling after a few short miles behind the wheel of any Porsche.

Contemporary Porsche advertisements state a simple criterion that has defined the marque since its inception in the 1940s: excellence. From the first Volkswagen-based model right up to today's fabulous Boxster, every model has borne the indelible stamp of excellence, both in design and state-of-the-art engineering.

Ferdinand Porsche's initial success came at the behest of Adolf Hitler, at the time when Hitler was just beginning his political rise to power in the 1930s. Dr. Porsche was commissioned by the führer to design a "people's car" (*ein Volkswagen*)—a car that would be at once affordable and inexpensive to operate for a population ravaged by economic depression. The performance parameters were simple: the car had to be able to travel on the autobahn at 60 miles per hour (95kph). Dr. Porsche visited the United States and observed the assembly plants and techniques that were capable of turning out more than fifty cars per hour. In meetings with Henry Ford, Porsche tried to interest Ford in the concept of the "people's car." Henry Ford, of course, scoffed at the idea—big cars were the big sellers in the United States—and Dr. Porsche returned to Germany to develop the car himself. That car became the now legendary Beetle—an economical car built for the everyday driver. But the design of the Beetle—with its rounded body and air-cooled engine configuration, situated strangely in the rear of the car—would become the foundation for the early Porsche sports cars and all subsequent models for decades afterward.

Roadsters were an integral part of Porsche's model lineup from the outset, up until the time they disappeared from the manufacturer's lineup in the mid-1960s (although not for the reasons most other roadsters would vanish a decade later). Porsche released the forever classic 911 in 1964, and from then on Porsches offered the top-down driving experience via Targa roofs. While convertibles were offered in the 911 line, as a two-plus-two car (albeit a small one), the 911 does not qualify as a true roadster. The 911's predecessors, though, the famous 356 series, were

offered as roadsters and were, in their time, some of the finest-handling and -performing roadsters ever built.

The 1947 356, designed by Ferdinand's son, Ferdinand "Ferry" Porsche, Jr., was the company's first true sports car. This car was sold to a wealthy Swiss who was so enamored by the car's performance he commissioned a road test on the car, which was reported in a magazine. The road test created much interest in the 356; so much, in fact, that an initial production run of fifty aluminum-bodied cars was planned.

The 356 was a two-seat roadster body on a VW floor pan. A tuned version of the standard 1131 cc VW flat-four powered the new roadster, named the Gmund after the town in Austria where the first run of fifty handmade 356s was manufactured in an old, unused lumber mill. However, the need for higher capacity resulted in production moving back to Stuttgart, Germany; there, subsequent 356s were manufactured with steel rather than the aluminum bodies that had characterized the initial run. By 1951 the five hundredth 356 was rolling off the assembly line; just three months later, a Porsche 356 came in twentieth place at the 24 Hours of Le

Mans. This finish at Le Mans was the start of a brilliant history that would see decades of Porsche involvement leading up to an overall win in 1970 with the incredible and wickedly fast 917 at the infamous Sarthe circuit. The philosophy that would become the hallmark of Porsche to the this day—*"designed for and proven on the track in competition"*—had begun. Engineering, the best possible, was at the core of all Porsche designs.

Ferdinand Porsche died in 1952 and the company passed into the hands of his son, Ferry, who had been running it since his father's imprisonment after World War II. The 356 continued in production until 1964. Like all Porsches, the car evolved throughout its run. Improvements were made over the years, with increases in all aspects of performance being the prime objective. Even during the heady decades of planned obsolescence throughout the auto industry during midcentury, Porsche never made changes based solely on aesthetics. Engine displacement in the 356 rose to 1500 ccs and then 1600 ccs. A coupe became available, and the success of Porsche overseas in the United States saw sales and the Porsche mystique grow.

In 1953 the first Carrera, a specially tuned 356, made its appearance. The name Carrera from that point on would be used only on special high-performance Porsche models, which became the most coveted of all Porsches, right on through the entire 911 production.

The 356A was introduced in 1955 and ran for four years. A Carrera model and a new, more powerful Speedster version with a 1600 cc engine appeared in '58. The 356B/Carrera 2 made its appearance in '59. Restyled, albeit subtly compared to the garish changes most cars went through at the time, the 356B continued the Porsche reputation of quality, performance, and success in sports car racing.

The 356C, introduced in 1963, would be the final incarnation of the 356. The C was the first production model to use discs all around, something of an anomaly for Porsche, even though by that time many manufacturers had been offering high-performance cars with discs all around for years. Performance was improved further but basically all that could be gotten out of an outdated, four-cylinder, rear-engine car had been done. The new replacement model, the 901, which became the incredible

OPPOSITE: *A 1959 Porsche Speedster. The year 1959 saw the end of the 356A. Ahead lay the 356B, improved and rare Carreras, and, in 1964, the beginning of Porsche's longest-running model, the ever-fabulous 911.*

ABOVE: *The 1955 Porsche Spyder unfortunately gained fame for being the car in which film idol James Dean died, rather than for being the cutting-edge, high-performance roadster that it was. On the track at the 24 Hours of Le Mans in 1955 the 550 Spyder garnered first place in the 1.5-liter class, took second in the 1.1-liter class, and won the prestigious Index of Performance award. The rich histories of Le Mans and Porsche would forever be intertwined, culminating with the incredible 917's outright win in 1970.*

ABOVE: **By 1988, the 911 had been in production for almost a quarter of a century. Constant refinement, based on lessons learned on the track, kept the car well ahead of competitors. The Cabriolet, German for "convertible," offered blistering performance with zero to sixty times in the low six-second range. With the top down, the wondrous sound of the flat six at peak revs could not have been sweeter.**

OPPOSITE TOP: **With a reverent nod to its lineage—the 550 Spyders—and a glimpse into the millennium with avant-garde technology and performance, the retrostyled Boxster is all Porsche.**

OPPOSITE BOTTOM: **Germany is home to some of the finest aftermarket tuners of Porsches in the world. Firms like Ruf and Strosek take delivery of new cars from the Porsche factory and work their magic for those Porschephiles for whom cost is no object and for whom a mere factory-spec model would never suffice. This 1994 Strosek-modified Speedster shows strong 356-series-inspired design, finished with Strosek wheels, exhaust tips, and others of the firm's signature modifications.**

911 when put into production, was already in advanced stages of design when the 356 entered its final years.

The 356 remains to this day a desirable Porsche. Current prices at major auctions like Barrett Jones in Phoenix have seen much interest in the 356, especially the Carrera and Speedster models. Decades after they contested at Le Mans, Porsche 356s continue to be a staple in SCCA club racing and vintage racing events across the country.

Porsche, though lacking a true roadster in the 911 line, would become one of the leading marques in sports cars. Its proven track record of performance is second to none.

As we will see in the final chapter, Porsche has returned to its roots in a sense with the development of its latest model, the Boxster. A true roadster, the Boxster is perhaps the finest retro design currently available from any manufacturer, combining the design heritage of the 356 series with the high-end engineering of the 911 series. It is packaged at an attractive price as compared to the wildly expensive 911 series, and it is one of the cars that assures the roadster will be around for decades to come.

BMW

Bayerische Motor Werkern, better known as Bavarian Motor Works or simply BMW, was originally a manufacturer of aircraft engines and motorcycles. Prior to World War II, BMW produced its first automotive design and in its time one of the finest sports cars available, the 328. After the war, the company began producing small, three-wheeled microcars for a cash-strapped and war-ravaged population. It was not until the 1960s that BMW began to produce the type of cars that would come to define the tradition of engineering and performance associated with all BMW cars today.

BMW got onto the roadster map in the late 1950s. The 507, produced between 1956 and 1959, remains legendary, perhaps in part because of its low production volume. Designed by Count Albrecht Goertz, this little roadster was built on a shortened 503 coupe chassis. A torquey small-block V-8 produced a respectable 150 horsepower. In spite of a design that was stunning, sales were not anything that one would refer to as even marginally successful. Production ceased in 1959 with just over 250 units manufactured and sold.

It would be almost thirty years before BMW produced another roadster, the Z-1. By then, BMW's reputation for "German engineering and race-bred performance" had been set in stone. The fiberglass-bodied Z-1, expensive and possessing styling gimmicks such as sliding doors that disappeared into the sills, never quite lived up to the initial excitement exhibited when it was shown as a concept car. Its successor, though, the BMW Z-3, introduced in 1995 and built in the United States, would prove to be the most successful roadster this German firm ever produced.

THIS PAGE: *Noted Italian designer Giovanni Michelotti took a stock BMW 507 roadster produced between 1956 and 1959 and performed a one-off styling exercise, hoping BMW would produce his model instead of the current 507. Despite a Vignale-built body, and a sleek, modern look for the period, BMW dropped the 507 after a poor sales run.*

OPPOSITE: *The M series BMWs have always been a cut above the stock models. While the initial Z-3 roadster had been a resounding success for the automaker, the BMW cognoscenti knew a wait would bear high-quality fruit. The M roadster, with a tuned six-cylinder, provided increased power and better handling in a more macho body.*

Chapter **SEVEN**

ROADSTER REVIVAL

f the 1970s were indeed the darkest days for roadsters, then the bright light reflecting off the finish of exciting new models displayed in showrooms and on the drawing boards in the new millennium is almost blinding. Some twenty-odd years after the roadster was essentially given up for dead by carmakers and buyers alike, the choice among roadsters is as overwhelming it is thrilling. It seems that no sooner is a new roadster released by one company—usually with rave reviews from both the automotive press and eager customers on the showroom floors—

than rumors run rampant of yet another new roadster in the pipeline from yet another carmaker.

New technology has enabled manufacturers to produce sports cars that are fuel-efficient, safe, and easier on the environment than anything previously offered. Factor in a robust economy and a huge customer base of middle-aged baby boomers with plenty of disposable income and a nostalgic longing for the cars they drooled over in their youth, and you've got one of the hottest and most stimulating new car markets the world has ever known.

JAPAN CHANGES THE ROADSTER GAME

While certainly not major players in the initial postwar decades of roadster design, it was the Japanese who were responsible for producing one of the finest and most affordable sports cars of the early 1970s, the Datsun 240-Z, introduced in 1969. Until the Z, affordable *and* dependable sports cars were not the norm. Yes, you usually could have one or the other, but rare was the sports car—be it a coupe or a roadster—that not only gave you a lot of bang for the buck but was reliable enough to be an everyday driver with minimal routine maintenance. The 240-Z delivered both aspects in spades: for a fair price, it offered styling that looked more Maranello Italian than Pacific Rim, and it outperformed everything else in its class.

The Z, while not a roadster, set down parameters that would become the hallmark of the Japanese auto industry: fantastic build quality, reliability that was second to none, fine performance, and an economy of ownership that ultimately changed and dictated the shape of the entire global auto industry. Gone were the days when American cars were the yardstick by which all other makes were judged. With the Z, Datsun stated that the Japanese had arrived as far as performance cars were concerned.

The Japanese auto industry, at that time known primarily for small economy sedans, had with the introduction of the Z come to the performance table with the main course. Over the coming decades, Japanese firms like Nissan (which, ironically, had used the Datsun pseudonym to avoid shaming the Nissan name should their venture into the auto industry fail), Honda, and Toyota would redefine Japan's role in the auto industry with successful sports cars, luxury models, and even trucks. But it was another company, Mazda, that brought back the roadster.

THE MIATA ARRIVES

The Mazda firm dates to the 1920s, but it was not involved in automobile manufacturing until late 1960. From 1960 on, Mazda produced a line of small two- and four-door economy sedans for the car-hungry home market.

In 1961 Mazda took a step that set them on the road to performance automobiles. They obtained a license from German automaker N.S.U. to manufacture the new rotary engine for their own line of cars. While the design was initially plagued by seal problems that leaked oil into the rotary chamber, Mazda engineers fixed the trouble and developed the design into a reliable and high-performing engine. The rotary or "wankel" engine found a home in a few sedans, but more importantly in the RX-7, a line of two-seat sports cars that offered value and high performance. The mixture of high performance and moderate pricing made sense, and Mazda continued to build its line in this direction. By the late 1980s the RX-7 had evolved into a serious sports car, and Mazda earned a solid reputation with it and a number of quality sedans as well.

To the higher-ups at Mazda, it seemed natural that this blend of value and performance would lend itself perfectly to a roadster, in the spirit of the classic British roadsters MG and Triumph. In the mid-1980s, the decision was made to introduce a roadster to the Mazda line. Known in the early phases of its development as the MX-5, this roadster was inspired by the Lotus Elan, which by then was generally considered the pinnacle of small roadster design. That car's Chapman-designed suspension and twin-cam, four-cylinder powerplant offered a contemporary level of performance in spite of its age. Mazda's new roadster, released in 1989 and renamed the Miata, bore a striking resemblance to the Elan in terms of both style and performance. Side by side, the Miata looked as though it were an updated, upgraded Elan developed by Lotus itself—it was a perfect homage to that legendary and classic roadster, gracefully updated for the '90s.

Of course, pundits remarked that once again the Japanese had done what they do best—that is, copied someone else's car. Mazda made no false pretenses with the Miata, however, and proudly let it be known up front that the car was based on the wonderful Elan. That fact alone excited roadster enthusiasts worldwide; the Miata's low initial price coupled with the now legendary Japanese reliability made the car into an overnight success.

Once given the chance to do drive reports on it, the worldwide automotive press was wildly enthusiastic about the Miata. And the buying public, perhaps harboring a pent-up longing for the traditional roadster that had been missing from automakers' lineups for so many years, created a demand that far outstripped initial production.

Grinning dealers had a field day, much like dealers of the first 240-Zs some twenty years earlier, and price gouging became common as demand exceeded supply on the initial run. No matter; if one customer wasn't willing to pay the inflated price, there was a line of wide-eyed hopefuls right behind with hard cash to pay for a taste of the open-road motoring they'd dreamed of for decades. And in the corporate headquarters of competing companies around the world, eyebrows were raised. Within a few years, the design studios of virtually every major automaker were knee-deep in designs that would redefine the conventional roadster. Blending conventional styling and performance goals with cutting-edge technology, a new breed of two-seat convertibles was set to follow in the Miata's wake.

The results have been staggering. The seemingly overnight success of this neat little roadster opened the floodgates worldwide, as manufacturers scrambled to add a roadster to their line of automobiles in order to meet the public's apparently insatiable demands for that most unique of driving experiences.

MORE OPEN-AIR FUN FROM THE LAND OF THE RISING SUN

In the twenty-first century, Japan continues to surprise and excite those who dream of a roadster. Competing companies have created high-performing and reasonably priced sports cars that are both appealing and accessible.

The Honda S-2000 takes the roadster experience to a new level. Using engineering gleaned from years of Formula One experience and world championships, Honda has created a most remarkable automobile. Pulling a whopping 240 horsepower out of a 2-liter four-cylinder engine is an engineering marvel, especially when this engine revs freely to a 9000 rpm redline. At $32,000 the S is affordable, but low production volume will make this a car that will quickly become rare as demand far exceeds its supply—and finding one at $32K will certainly be a challenge then.

Toyota is hot on Honda's heels with a new roadster in the planning stages, and Mazda continues to improve its now classic Miata, which remains true to the tradition of Great Britain's finest roadsters.

GERMANY TAKES THE HIGH-END ROAD

While Japan has placed a lock on the affordable roadster market, German firms continue to set their sights on the luxury-minded buyers with a bevy of pricey yet priceless two-seaters that live up to the German tradition of unbeatable performance and engineering.

BMW Goes Retro

Hard on the heels of the Miata came the BMW Z-3 in 1995. Strikingly beautiful, the Z-3 was a combination of retrostyling cues from the previous 507 roadster coupled with the macho, no-nonsense look of their celebrated finely crafted and engineered sedans. Priced above the Miata, the Z-3 provided all that BMW was famous for: performance, engineering, and German build quality. If there was one downside to the car, it was the four-cylinder engine initially offered, which simply was not up to the task of fast motoring associated with a car of the Z-3's style or price. Its lackluster four-cylinder was replaced first with a six and then a full-blown M series version. The M, which stands for BMW Motorsports, is a special tag reserved for those offerings that feature higher performance and handling than the off-the-shelf models; to true BMW aficionados, the M Series, whether a sedan or roadster, is the peak of BMW design and performance.

At the upper end of the BMW line is the soon-to-be-released and all-new Z-8 roadster. The lucky owners of the Z-8, which is priced at more than $120,000, will not have to worry about seeing similar cars either in the rearview mirror or coming at them on any road, as extremely low production numbers and a very high sticker price will make this a rare BMW indeed. Underhood is a neck-snapping 400 horsepower thirty-two-valve V-8 engine, coupled with a six-speed Getrag transmission. A Formula One–style, steering-wheel-mounted sequential shifter will be available as an option. That, along with a drive-by-wire throttle—which is wired directly into the computer that manages the engine, rather than via the more traditional cable attached to the carburetors of the fuel-injection unit—will make the Z-8 BMW's high-tech statement for the new millennium.

BMW boldly claims that the Z-8's only real competition will come from the Porsche 911 Turbo, Mercedes Vision SLR, and the Ferrari 360—the veritable top of the performance sports cars food chain. Styling is BMW's most retro effort to date: in appearance, the Z-8 seems to have sprung naturally from the BMW 507 roadster of the 1950s, as though the original roadster never went out of production but has evolved organically over the ensuing decades into the masterpiece that will hit BMW showrooms in the spring of 2001.

RIGHT: *While the first Z-3 roadster, powered by a four-cylinder engine, was an immediate market success for BMW, the firm's fans knew that their patience would be rewarded. And it was: the M roadster delivered Z performance to match its handsome, retro-507-inspired body. The M Division upgrades give bigger brakes, more tuned suspension, and flared fenders to accommodate the fat Z-rated seventeen-inch tires and wheels. The real M jewel is the engine, a silky-smooth six that pumps out 240hp.*

PORSCHE'S BEAUTIFUL BOXSTER

With the roadster market blossoming, Porsche stepped into the ring with the sum total of all they had learned over decades at venues such as Le Mans, Daytona, Sebring, and the Targa Florio. While the 911 continued to thrive with a new and highly anticipated model released in 1998, the famed German firm was also busily preparing for the introduction of its new and exciting roadster, a near-perfect two-seater called the Boxster. A true roadster, the Boxster caught the attention of enthusiasts everywhere, and at half the price of a 911 it is actually within reach of many of them.

Like BMW's Z-3, the Boxster was a retro design, in this case borrowing from the competition RSKs of the '50s while incorporating the sleek elegance of modern-day German styling and engineering. Its midengine design gave an almost perfect 50/50 front and rear weight balance, and made for exceptionally fine handling. The engine was water-cooled (a first for Porsche), and the Boxster was the first car the automaker offered that had a sealed engine compartment—which meant that aside from

checking vital fluid levels, engine maintenance could be attended to only by qualified Porsche mechanics. For model year 2000, Porsche released the Boxster S, a more powerful and higher-performing version of the base car.

AUDI SHAKES THINGS UP

German maker Audi has earned a solid reputation for its high-performance all-wheel-drive Quattro sedans and a line of fine luxury sedans. In 1998 Audi entered the sports car market with its daring TT coupe. Designed in the United States, in southern California, by the same creative and outside-the-box stylist that penned the new Volkswagen Beetle, the TT looks like nothing else on the road.

Inspired by the prewar German Bauhaus school of design, the TT is the strongest retro statement yet to roll on four wheels. This stunning and user-friendly roadster would be equally at home zipping through a futuristic landscape or heading out for a day's drive over backcountry roads. With the TT, Germany has regained its lead role in automotive design, setting standards and styling cues for the coming decade.

OPPOSITE: *With the S package, the already spectacular Porsche Boxster gets a boost in performance that brings it ever closer to its more expensive sibling, the 911. Its 250hp gets to the road through a six-speed gearbox, while its water-cooled six, mounted midships for perfect weight distribution, delivers the fine handling that makes it most entertaining to drive.*

ABOVE: *The Boxster cabin is pure Porsche: the gauges are arranged to be read at a glance, the controls are at the driver's fingertips, and the gear lever is perfectly placed to snick up and down as quickly as possible. The Boxster is one of those rare sports cars that actually increases the driver's skill level.*

LEFT: *Porsche builds what may be the most powerful and aggressive brakes ever mounted behind a Z-rated tire. The marque's longtime and well-deserved reputation is upheld by the braking ability of both the Boxster S, whose vented rotors are seen here, and the 911.*

The startling design elements of the TT have been studied and copied, and have found their way onto everything from the Mitsubishi GT to the new Ford "World Car," the Focus. This author first saw the TT at the New York Auto Show a few years back, when it was still in its design study phase. So different and so compelling was the design that I found myself returning to the Audi exhibit time and time again. Each time I looked at the car, it was like seeing it for the first time. That year was my first visit to the New York show and I cannot now remember any other car.

Also available as a coupe, the TT roadster benefits from the added thrill of a soft top; indeed, the coupe pales in comparison. As an option, the leather interior is available with baseball glove–styled stitching. Clearly, creativity in the TT design reached a new zenith.

MERCEDES PUTS THE TOP DOWN

While Mercedes always had an SL roadster in its line, that car was more luxury than performance, a bit large with a sticker price to match. In 1996 Mercedes answered the demand, and released its stunning SLK roadster.

Smaller in size and lower in price than the SL series of roadsters, the SLK in no time had a two-year waiting list for delivery. In place of the traditional cloth "roadster" top, Mercedes engineered a steel roof that retracted into the trunk. Peak performance came from an optional supercharged engine, noted by the tasteful, almost understated badge on the front fenders announcing *KOMPRESSOR*.

Mercedes has temptingly dangled for all to see what an entry-level roadster in the Mercedes line might look like in the years to come. Called the Vision SLA, this bold roadster—even as a styling exercise—is unlike any other car. A foot shorter than the SLK, this marvel is made of plastic composites and aluminum. Viewed from the front it looks as if the nose of Mikka Hakkinen's world champion Formula One McLaren (powered by Mercedes) has been flattened out, its wings tucked into slots on the fenders and glued to the hood. The interior? "Different" is a gross understatement. Minimal in appointments, its radical design will be a controversial proposition at best. If it does find its way into production, expect this Formula One–inspired Mercedes roadster to have a waiting list longer than that of the SLK.

THE UNITED STATES AND GREAT BRITAIN

With successful roadsters speeding out of Germany and Japan, it was only a matter of time before carmakers in England—the traditional home of the classic roadster—and the United States caught on and developed sleek little two-seaters of their own.

MEANWHILE, BACK IN THE U.K. . . .

With life-saving infusions of capital from proud new parent Ford, Jaguar continued their rich roadster tradition, set down by the XKE, with the 1999 XKR luxury roadster. A further development of the XJ8 roadster, the XKR pumps out a respectable 370 horsepower from a supercharged 4-liter V-8 engine. At more than $84,000, the XKR is not a car for the masses. However, those who can afford to put this stylish and high-performing cat in their climate-controlled garage can rest assured, knowing that their ride is no newcomer: the XKR comes from one of the finest and richest lineages in roadster history. For the budget-minded enthusiast,

OPPOSITE: *Mercedes's SLK roadster, with its retractable hardtop, allows you to drive year-round in sedan comfort; with the optional supercharged engine you get stellar performance, on top of classic Mercedes craftsmanship and longevity.*

BELOW: *Aimed squarely at buyers of the Mercedes SL roadsters, this 1999 Jaguar XKR offers 370 supercharged hp at your foot. The elegance of English burled wood and leather throughout the interior makes the XKR a perfect blend of XKE-style performance and the understated luxury of Jaguar's fine line of sedans.*

there is the normally aspirated (sans supercharger) XJ8 roadster, priced in the slightly more moderate $56,000 range.

The roadster has been revived at Lotus as well. Continuing in the rich tradition of the Elan, Lotus in 1996 introduced a lightweight and high-load, G-force cornering, slot car–like roadster, the sexy Elise. Embodying all that Colin Chapman decreed necessary for a car to be considered a Lotus—a small, high-revving, and torquey engine, a state-of-the-art suspension that makes the car run as though it were on rails, and a light weight—the Elise is believed by many to be the best roadster to come out of England in decades.

THE NEW AMERICAN ROADSTERS

The U.S. auto industry is unique. As the millennium turned, American carmakers were busily catering to a buying public enamored with pickup trucks and gargantuan sport utility vehicles that twenty years ago were referred to as commercial delivery trucks. Now these heavy haulers, festooned in leather and cup holders galore, deliver kids to playing fields and play bumper cars in shopping-mall parking lots, all to the tune of a paltry twelve to fourteen miles (19–23km) per gallon.

But the sports car is not dead in the United States. The success of tiny, fun imports like the Mazda Miata and the new Volkswagen Beetle has sent the Big Three a clear message: for every baby boomer looking for a big, child-friendly, and environmentally unfriendly SUV or minivan, there's one looking for a piece of his or her own past, in addition to the young Generation X-er who just wants something cool to drive.

The Corvette, of course, has staunchly held its own through waves of change in the auto industry, and remains America's one true sports car. Recently redesigned from the ground up, the Corvette continues to carry on the tradition laid down way back in the early '50s. Beautiful in terms of both looks and performance, the 2000 Corvette is a roadster to be reckoned with. (See the Afterword for a drive report on the stunning Corvette C-5.)

OPPOSITE AND ABOVE: *A Lotus in every way that makes Lotus legendary, the Elise is probably one of the best-handling cars available today. The Lotus roadster experience will once again thrill those who know Chapman's legacy. There is a hint of Austin-Healey Bugeye charm in the smiling front end of this wild child.*

LEFT: *This otherwise macho 1994 Dodge Viper has an almost feminine air of grace and civility about it. Don't be fooled though—for raw power in the manner of 1960s American muscle cars, the Viper has no equal.*

OPPOSITE: *In the tradition of Shelby and Chapparal, the Viper is the true heir of the American sports cars. Stuff the biggest and most powerful engine under the hood, tune the suspension for handling, put the top down, hit the gas, and feel the Gs throw you back into the seat like few cars can.*

DODGE LETS LOOSE THE VIPER

In 1992 Dodge released a roadster that once and for all put to rest the image of the K Car and the Caravan minivan: the wild and wicked Viper. The brainchild of Chrylser president Bob Lutz, the car was conceived to be a present-day Shelby, priced at less than $100,000.

The RT-10 Viper roadster hit the market with a price tag of $72,000. With a whopping 400 horsepower pouring out of a V-10 engine, the Viper was an immediate success. Lacking the refinement and high-tech appeal of contemporary offerings of the time, the Viper appealed to the U.S. ideal of raw horsepower wrapped in an exciting body. Throw it into gear, mash down the accelerator, and take off like a bullet. Although the body's fit, finish, and handling did not initially match the power it produced, a recent redesign has refined the car while at the same time, through racing experience, improving its overall performance and handling. Chrysler-Daimler has turned the Viper into a world-class sports car. Few roadsters offer the wind in your face at the hurricane-gale-rate a Viper can.

THE THUNDERBIRD FLIES AGAIN

When Ford discontinued the Thunderbird in 1989, many T-Bird enthusiasts were heartbroken. Some, though, felt an odd sense of relief, noting that the only true T-Bird was the original two-seat roadster offered from 1955 through '57. Fans of those early Birds were thrilled when Ford announced that it was bringing back the Thunderbird, and that the new model—slated for debut in 2001 or 2002—would be a ground-up redesign, retrostyled to echo the lines and format of those first-generation T-Birds.

The car was first shown at the 1999 New York Auto Show and was hands down the domestic hit of the show. Returning to the roadster design concept that made those early models legendary in popularity, the new T-Bird will be a masterful blend of retrostyling cues of those early Birds combined with the vanguard technology that Ford has embraced over the past decade and a half. The new Thunderbird will be built on the midsize Lincoln LS platform, and that bodes well for the performance image long absent from the Thunderbird: the LS has received accolades from the motoring press for its fine performance and handling, drawing comparisons to BMW's 3 and 5 series.

Initial plans call for the Thunderbird to be powered by a 3.9-liter 32-valve V-8 engine putting out a respectable 252 horsepower. Getting that power to the wheels will be through a five-speed automatic transmission, and projected performance figures based on the LS would yield zero-to-sixty figures in the high six-second range. And with Jaguar now within the Blue Oval of parent Ford, there is speculation that the twin supercharged V-8 that powers the new Jaguar XKR along with a six-speed manual may find itself in the Bird down the line. After far too long an absence, the roadster experience will once again roll out the doors of your local Ford dealership.

PANOZ: A NEW AMERICAN INDEPENDENT

There have been many would-be new carmakers whose light shone bright at the outset only to tailspin and burn out after a short period, Brooklin and DeLorean being the most recent examples. Then there are those rare ones like Carroll Shelby who seem to do everything right, and to whom success seems to come easily. In the competitive global automotive market, only a few independent manufacturers have been able to come close to the success that Shelby achieved in the 1960s. One of them is the United States' newest roadster manufacturer, Panoz.

Don Panoz is one of those self-starting and self-made men who make great covers and copy in the pages of *Fortune* magazine. Panoz directed the profits of his remunerative invention—the stop-smoking patch—into his true passion: cars and racing. He subscribed to the simple concept behind some of the greatest U.S. roadsters: that a big, powerful V-8 driving the rear wheels and a fine-tuned suspension and brakes to match the performance were the key to great cars.

The Panoz roadster, released in 1989, is a throwback to those early postwar MGs in its style. Front fenders are mounted separate from the body, headlights are stand-alones in gleaming chrome nacelles, much like the early MGs and 1930s prewar designs. Mechanically, the car uses off-the-shelf Ford Mustang components, including a 305-horsepower 4.6-liter V-8. Handcrafted of aluminum, the sleek body provides a low weight-to-power ratio, and its performance is dazzling. Unlike the similarly styled Morgan, which continues to successfully produce with outdated mechanicals, the Panoz roadster combines traditional sports car design with modern high-tech engineering. Low in production, high in price, the Panoz is like no other contemporary car on the road.

More modern, slightly more mainstream in appearance, and higher priced than the roadster is the Esperante, the second roadster to arrive from Panoz. As with the first, performance is foremost in the Esperante. Using Ford engines, chassis components, and firewall, the Esperante offers a first-class roadster experience. Like Jaguars, Austin-Healeys, and Porsches, Panoz cars are race-proven on long-distance circuits—Le Mans, Daytona, and Sebring. The design heritage and glorious history of roadsters are embodied in every Panoz.

OPPOSITE: *The retrostyling of the soon-to-be-released Ford Thunderbird is an homage to the roadster Birds of 1955 through 1957. Offering two seats only, in the spirit of the original roadsters, this new Thunderbird adds the Ford oval to the growing ranks of fine new open cars hitting the open road.*

LEFT: *With proven Ford vanguard mechanicals inside, the hybrid A.I.V. Panoz, introduced in 1994, might just be the reincarnation of the Lotus Seven for the new millennium: fantastic performance in an elegantly styled, if minimalist package.*

AFTERWORD
A DRIVE REPORT ON THE CORVETTE C-5

The week before I met my first Corvette C-5, I had finished reading James Schefter's fascinating book, *All Corvettes Are Red*, an in-depth look at the new C-5 Corvette. Schefter had been granted unlimited access to go where few had gone before—behind the scenes at General Motors to witness firsthand how a car is developed, from concept to the showroom floor.

Few if any enthusiasts get to witness the evolution of a new car from concept through design and development, right up to its momentous release. Schefter was invited in during a pivotal time in the Corvette's history: in the early 1990s, a struggling GM was doing a corporate slash and burn to reduce costs and maintain its status as a major player in the worldwide automotive market, and the low-volume and costly Corvette was a ripe target for President Robert C. Stempel's ax. Yet despite some close calls, in 1997 the Corvette reemerged from the corporate rubble like the mythical phoenix in the form of the fabulous C-5.

Rather than a restyled and haphazard update on the then current but seriously outdated C-4, the new Corvette was an entirely different animal—from the ground up, it was every bit as fine as any of the best sports cars the world over. Against overwhelming odds, the Corvette had not only survived, it had been transformed into a driving statement, asserting that the United States can engineer and build a sports cars as fine as those of Stuttgart, Maranello, or Coventry.

And here I was with Mr. Schefter's incredible story alive in my hands and at my feet as I sat behind the wheel of a brand-spankin'-new 1999 Corvette C-5 (red, of course). Alongside a good friend who happened to be the editor of *Vette* magazine, I was headed out for a daylong drive report in order to feature this new C-5. We planned a route from northwest New Jersey, through Pennsylvania to Scranton, and back. On a perfect spring day, it was top down all the way.

From the outside, the C-5 displayed a contemporary silhouette while still paying due homage to the rich lineage of the marque with its sweeping, sensual styling cues. The cockpit was state of the art—spacious yet intimate, like a roadster should be, the seat a perfect blend of torso-grabbing racing bucket and long-highway-trip comfort. The gauges were perfectly laid out across the expanse of black dash, the controls at the driver's fingertips. A few adjustments to the power-seat controls, and any driver could easily find a comfortable arms-out driving position. The engine springs to life and, in spite of more than 370 horsepower, the red C-5 rolled from a stop as smoothly and easily as a Honda sedan. Cruising west on Route 80 at 65 miles per hour (105kph), the tach showed 1100 revs. Loafing, perhaps, but the exquisite aluminum engine did not once announce its displeasure at the leisurely pace.

In Pennsylvania we headed onto Route 449, a mountain roadway full of twists, winds, and switchbacks nestled between straightaways of various lengths. It is a perfect road on which to test one's driving skills and to get a sense of just what a car can do, and the beautiful surroundings make it ideal for open-air motoring.

We drove onto a long, ascending straightaway that led into a sweeping, banked lefthander a half mile (0.8km) or so ahead with the accelerator pressed down—the "drive-by-wire" throttle response was instantaneous. In the tradition of all great American stump-pulling V-8s, we were pushed back into our seats, although the rumble, gear whine, and other explosive sounds associated with raw American V-8 power coming on the cam were pleasantly absent. The C-5 motor is silky smooth, the torque awesome, the exhaust note more European than aftermarket Thrush. Shifting is effortless, and the pedal placement is pure perfection.

On the throttle through the turn, the weight shifts, a fleeting reminder that the Corvette is a heavy car as the Goodyear rubber holds the line true. Exit the turn with the power on full, and the engine winds up as you rifle down a short straight into a tight righthander. So smooth and free revving is this marvelous engine that it feels like it can easily rev to 10,000 rpm—hence a rev limiter that cuts off the engine when the computer senses redline. Power on through the entire turn, and then the road leads to a long downhill straight into a series of S curves; full throttle downhill, third up to fourth. A glance at the speedo shows us edging over 90 mph (145kph); a hard downshift and a slam on the pedal reveals brakes comparable to those on a modern Porsche.

Never have I had such an exhilarating and, at the same time, relaxed experience behind the wheel of any car. Acceleration, handling, shifting, braking: the C-5 has truly world-class anchors. All these elements combine into a seamless and exciting driving experience. The C-5 transmits information so legibly and so immediately through the steering, pedals, and seat that you actually feel your driving skills improving as the miles roll by. It might be a cliché to state that you become one with the car, but that is the C-5 experience. The C-5 imparts a sense of confidence like few roadsters can, and it is like no other Corvette that has come before it. It stands alone as perhaps GM's greatest automotive achievement.

Reflecting on a similar Pennsylvania roadster experience almost a quarter of a century earlier—my thrilling ride behind the wheel of a Jaguar XKE at Pocono Raceway in 1976—I am astounded by technology's progress in such a short blip on the time line. The XKE was the very definition of a classic postwar British roadster. It was from an entirely different world, one where more was required of any driver to get all of what the Jaguar was capable of offering, and my skills were certainly not up to that task. It was nonetheless a fantastic experience, albeit frustrating and at some moments even scary. But such was not the case with the C-5.

The C-5 roadster ranks as one of the finest cars I have had the pleasure of driving. In truth, I've never been a big fan of Corvettes (beyond the '63 split-window coupe)—until now. Never has so much performance, speed, and stimulation been crafted and packaged in such a finely engineered manner. And the added sensual pleasure of the top-down roadster leaves me wondering why anyone would order a hardtop and miss out on the wind, the wonderful exhaust note, and the blue sky above.

Be they the skinny-tired, high-fendered MGs and Triumphs of yesteryear or today's engineering marvels like the C-5, TT, Boxster, and SLK, there is simply nothing like being at the wheel of a roadster. What all roadsters have in common is that intimate, wind-in-your-face driving experience that other styles of automobile simply cannot offer. With their history of glamour and performance, they summarize a century.

It is chilling to think back to those dark days of the 1970s and ponder the fact that the roadster was almost relegated to the boneyard. These uniquely pleasurable machines might have gone the way of the woodie, existing only as classic and antique cars that proud owners take out for fleeting weekend rides or share with others in fields of parked cars at weekend shows. Instead, the sheer love, indeed, longing for the roadster experience stretched the imagination and technical skills of a new generation of automotive engineers and designers, many of whom were perhaps at one time touched by an old MG, a Jaguar, or Triumph and never forgot the thrill. Happily, the end of the century has seen the roadster redefined and reshaped, and available in the form of some of the finest machines ever to hit the road. The roadster has returned, and this time it is here to stay.

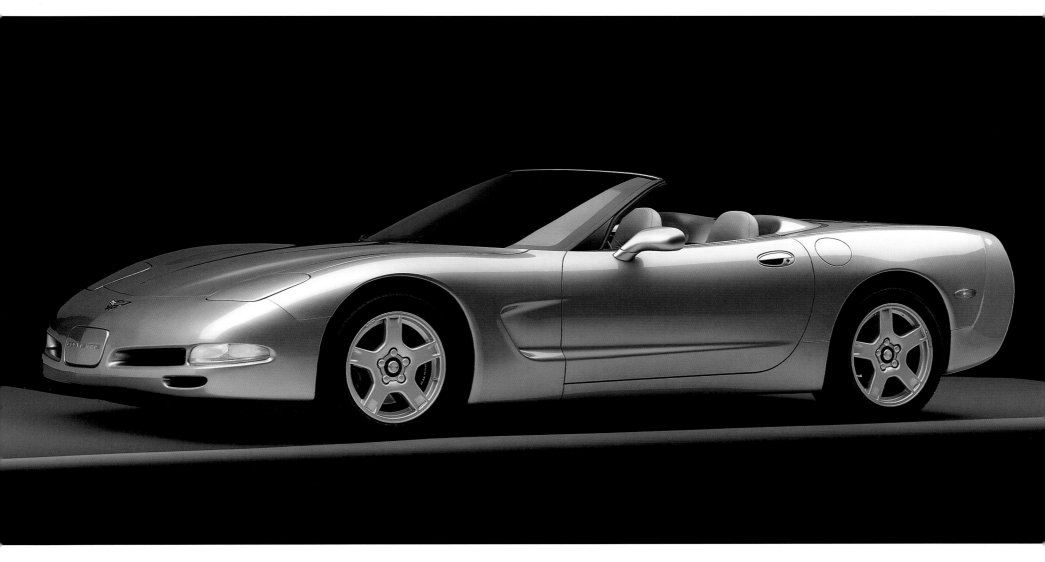

ABOVE: *The new Corvette C-5 is a true, world-class sports car. Totally innovative from the ground up, this roadster for the third millennium fuses cutting-edge engineering, performance, and handling in a design that pays refined tribute to the all-American Corvette legacy.*

PHOTO CREDITS